THE SANTA BARBARA B-24 DISASTERS

THE SANTA BARBARA B-24 DISASTERS

A CHAIN OF TRAGEDIES ACROSS AIR, LAND & SEA

ROBERT A. BURTNESS

Charleston   London

THE
History
PRESS

Published by The History Press
Charleston, SC 29403
www.historypress.net

Copyright © 2012 by Robert A. Burtness
All rights reserved

First published 2012

Manufactured in the United States

ISBN 978.1.60949.571.8

Library of Congress CIP data applied for.

Contents

CONTENTS

Acknowledgements

To the following, who provided invaluable information (often unobtainable anywhere else) for the preparation of this manuscript, I am indebted.

DUNCAN ABBOTT: He provided several color prints from the San Miguel Island crash site of B-24 Liberator, serial no. 42-7160. Further, it was his father-in-law, Robert "Bob" Brooks, who leased the island from the government for thirty-five years, beginning in 1913, and used it for a sheep ranching operation.

GEORGE C. BELITSKUS JR.: The eldest son of one of the crew members, he provided some interesting records about his father's military career.

DONNA BLAKE: John Wedesky's daughter, she provided further information about her late father's military experiences.

JOHN W. BRADFORD JR.: A former B-24 pilot who joined us during the investigation at the *Hat in the Ring* (or *Eddie Rickenbacker*) crash site, he helped to identify various parts of the plane and also provided some insight about what happened during the impact.

JOHN BRIDGWATER: Through his botanical knowledge, this former Los Padres National Forest district ranger located the main crash site of the *Hat in the Ring* Liberator.

Former B-24 pilot John Bradford was especially helpful in identifying various parts at the 42-0711 wreck site. In this photo, he is holding a waist machine gun mount. The guns themselves, as well as other sensitive equipment, were removed very shortly after the crash. *Photo by Bob Burtness.*

LYNN BURTNESS: The list of individuals providing significant help along the path of this pursuit would not be complete without recognizing my loving, supportive wife, Lynn. She not only offered useful suggestions during the manuscript preparation and proofreading process, but she also tolerated my frequent "disappearances" into the recess of our turreted Victorian library to interact with a sophisticated computer beneath an eighty-two-year-old wrought-iron chandelier.

TOM BUTERA: A longtime friend whom I have known since elementary school, he casually mentioned, in about 1980, a Liberator wreck in the Santa Barbara backcountry. A short time later, I visited what turned out to be the fringes of the wreck site and had trouble finding it on a subsequent trip. But at least my mission had begun and proceeded, albeit at a snail's pace. My procrastination was unfortunate because during the decade of the 1980s, there would have been more surviving crew members available to contact. This effort, however, would have been more challenging at that time since computers and the tools of the Internet were not developed nearly as much as they were later.

Jana Churchwell: She is the niece of Liberator pilot George F. Churchwell Jr., who died during a training flight crash in Weed, California, on June 10, 1943. Jana spent much time and effort seeking information and photos about the families of the Liberator crew members in this study, especially the crash in which her uncle died. A survivor of that crash was Lieutenant Douglas Thornburg, who died in the San Miguel Island crash only three weeks later.

Eugene Hartley: Now deceased, this retired San Marcos High School (one of three in what is now the Santa Barbara Unified School District) principal and former B-24 pilot provided some insight about the difficulties of maintaining proper fuel consumption in the Liberators. He also gave me a copy of a significant bibliographical resource that helped to move my research effort to the next level. I view his knowledge of Liberators as an extra benefit of our relationship. He also hired me to join his staff as an English teacher a decade before I realized that the remains of both plane wrecks were located within Santa Barbara County.

Steven Horne: A former Los Padres National Forest (LPNF) archaeologist, he headed the investigative work at the *Hat in the Ring* (or *Eddie Rickenbacker*) crash site and also located a copy of the Individual Fire Report in the LPNF archives.

Connie Johnson: The daughter of the pilot, she provided some details of her late father's flying experiences during the war, especially the first bailout over Santa Barbara. The last one to parachute from the aircraft after it cleared the coastal mountain range, he was the only crew member who landed in the upper Santa Ynez Valley.

Marc McDonald: His perseverance in digging up information, both text and photographs, from a variety of sources, including the children of some of the deceased crew members, significantly helped fill some gaps in this amazing story. His sharing of this information is deeply appreciated.

Gus Polasek: A B-17 pilot during World War II, he also had experience flying B-24s as a ferry pilot. Gus was also one of my interviewees in the Commemorative Air Force Oral History Program some time ago.

ACKNOWLEDGEMENTS

HAROLD E. PROVINCE: As treasurer and corresponding secretary of the Thirty-fourth Bomb Group Association, as well as a representative of the Eighth Air Force Historical Society, he contacted George C. Belitskus Jr., a member of the latter organization, who provided some background information about his late father's military career.

RAYMOND W. RICHART: As a longtime U.S. Forest Service radio technician and communications officer, he visited the Camuesa Canyon B-24 wreck site shortly after the crash and shared his views about the incident.

RAY RICHTER: A close friend, neighbor and fellow World War II veteran of John Wedesky's, he provided more details about John's experiences in China. Both men were members of the Eagles, a group of World War II veterans that gathered in their hometown of Janesville, Wisconsin, once a month to share their experiences and observations on a variety of topics.

JERRY ROBERTS: I would be remiss by not acknowledging History Press commissioning editor Jerry Roberts's help. He was not only willing to take a chance with an unknown writer, but he was also a patient, encouraging guide along the labyrinth of challenges from preparing the manuscript and images to the final step, publication. Adding this project to the others on his plate must relate in some way to being an air-traffic controller.

NANCY LORRAINE HASSINGER SNOW: Crew member Braydon Hassinger's daughter, she provided copies of photographs, newspaper articles and certificates about her late father.

GAIL VANLANDINGHAM: Located via a stroke of luck on the Internet, he was one of two living survivors of the original crew who told the story not only of the training flight from Salinas Army Air Base and the subsequent bailout over Santa Barbara but also how they spent the rest of the war flying missions from their China base, as well as about the second bailout and finding their way back to freedom. Gail is also the only crew member with whom I enjoyed a face-to-face interview, at his home in Everett, Washington.

JOHN WEDESKY: The second living survivor of the original crew (located with the help of Gail Vanlandingham), he shared his perspective of the bailouts and the escape from the Japanese-held territory in China.

Introduction

This is a story, but it is not intended to be a "war story." Instead, it is a tale of some young men who wanted to come to the aid of their country when its way of life and its very existence were in jeopardy.

It is a tale that tells a little bit about what their lives were like as civilians and what they were like in what was then called the United States Army Air Forces (USAAF)—when they experienced some very pleasant moments, when they endured some very uncomfortable ones and how their lives were sometimes endangered while they went about their business of doing what they were trained to do.

Some of them survived World War II, and some of them did not. All of them were on a mission to help, directly or indirectly, defeat the enemy and make life better for the existing and future generations back home. While appropriate recognition is always due to each of those warriors who served on the front lines on the ground, on the high seas or in the air, one must always remember the ten unknown and unseen individuals who supported the missions performed by each of these warriors.

Much time and effort has been made to tell this story as accurately as possible, but there are undoubtedly errors and inconsistencies. For example, facts and other information obtained from various sources do not always agree.

Further, the first-person accounts of the two living survivors, located after years of searching for them, were told more than half a century after the events happened; unlike what the camera lens sees, our recollections are subject to change.

Also, the second-person accounts obtained from a few of the children of the deceased crewmen are also subject to some "embroidering" of what really happened for the same reason. Reflecting on this topic in his later years, Mark Twain observed that he could "remember everything whether it happened or not."

Since I chose to attempt to tell this story in the interest of helping to preserve a bit of our local aviation history, though, any errors or omissions are my own responsibility and no one else's. I am fortunate to have found some documents that help to explain what happened and, of course, to have talked with two men who were there when these events occurred.

The B-24 Liberator and Its Variants

For some reason not fully understood, I have always been interested in aviation in general and World War II aviation in particular. Thus, when a friend told me about a B-24 Liberator crash site in our own county of Santa Barbara more than thirty years ago, I wanted to learn as much as possible about the circumstances behind this unique event. I call it "unique" because as far as I can determine, it is one of the two (or possibly three) largest plane wrecks in the history of our county. The first documented accident, by the way, led to the second Liberator loss only a few hours later, also in Santa Barbara County but on an offshore island.

From the first flight on December 29, 1939, to the end of production on May 31, 1945, more than 18,400 Liberators were built. This resulted in the B-24 flying more missions and dropping more bombs than any other World War II aircraft. Unlike the B-17s, it also flew in every theater of operations during the war.

Due to the high quantity requirements, they could not all be built at one location, or even by one manufacturer. Consequently, they were produced by the Consolidated Aircraft Corporation (later called Consolidated/ Vultee, or Convair, when the two companies merged in 1943) in Fort Worth, Texas, and San Diego, California; Douglas Aircraft in Tulsa, Oklahoma; North American Aviation in Dallas, Texas; and the Ford Motor Company at its newly built Willow Run, Michigan plant, which eventually produced 1 bomber per hour, or 650 per month, on its mile-long assembly line. According to one Liberator pilot, who accumulated forty-three combat missions, including some very dangerous ones over the Ploesti oil refineries in Romania, "the B-24s built at Willow Run were not as good as those built elsewhere."

At one point in its development, however, these bombers might have been B-17 "Flying Fortresses" and not B-24 Liberators at all. In October 1938, when Consolidated Aircraft was approached about setting up a second-source production line for the B-17, the offer was declined since Consolidated had moved to San Diego from Buffalo, New York, three years earlier and was preparing to enlarge its facilities. In addition, it was thought that the new Davis wing design, with its lower-drag feature, would contribute to the creation of a better bomber.

Unfortunately, the parts manufactured in these factories were not always interchangeable, and the constant changes in the various models created more problems in the production process. Modification centers were later established to upgrade the affected aircraft that may have just left the factories but were already obsolete.

While most of them were designed as various models of bombers, others were built to be transports (LB-30A and C-87, the latter of which became the first aircraft configured for use by the president of the United States), fuel tankers (C-109), trainers (TB-24), lead ships (CB-24) and photo-reconnaissance aircraft (F-7). These aircraft, plus the navy's PB4Y-1 Liberator, used for long-range submarine patrols, all had split tails.

However, another navy version, the PB4Y-2 Privateer, had a single tail. A land-based bomber, these were used for patrols, antisubmarine work and reconnaissance. Some were used during the Korean War, and a few were later employed as air tankers to fight forest fires until 2002, when one broke up in the air while fighting a fire near Estes Park, Colorado, on July 18 of that year. Both crew members were killed in that mishap.

Out of 977 produced, only 6 of them survive: 3 of them are airworthy but grounded in Greybull, Wyoming; 2 others are on display at the Yankee Air Force facility in Belleville, Michigan, and the National Museum of Naval Aviation in Naval Air Station Pensacola, Florida; and the last one is being restored at the Lone Star Flight Museum in Galveston, Texas.

The Liberator's wingspan, featuring the newly developed Davis wing, was 110 feet long. This facilitated a slightly greater speed, about three hundred miles an hour, and a longer range than the B-17 Flying Fortresses. At the same time, though, it necessitated a lower elevation ceiling, which in this case was at about thirty thousand feet, or about five thousand feet lower than that of the B-17. Heavier than the B-17, the B-24 was more difficult to fly, especially under adverse weather conditions.

A Chain of Tragedies across Air, Land and Sea

P4Y-2 Privateer air tanker. This aircraft, photographed at the Santa Barbara Airport, is similar to another air tanker, N7620C 123, which lost a wing during a fire near Estes Park, Colorado, on July 18, 2002. Both crew members were killed in the accident. *Photo by Bob Burtness.*

This new wing was named after David R. Davis, a freelance aeronautical engineer who ultimately convinced Consolidated to employ his design due to its advantages of lower drag and higher lift capabilities even at shallow angles of attack. Model and wing wind tunnel tests at the California Institute of Technology in Pasadena appeared to confirm these claims, and the design was used on both Consolidated's Model 31 Flying Boat, intended for both commercial and military (P4Y-1) use, and subsequently, the "secret bomber," which became the B-24.

While thousands of B-24s were built, only one Model 31 Flying Boat prototype was manufactured. Due to delays in building this prototype and a shortage of the ultimately unreliable Wright Duplex Cyclone engines, which were channeled toward production of the B-29 Superfortress, the order for two hundred of them, to be used for maritime patrol, was cancelled.

These highly efficient but thinner Davis wings, however, were potential problems in combat because they could break off if hit by enemy fire in critical structural locations. There is a photographic record of such an event happening on at least one occasion.

Eighteen tanks in these wings held 2,750 gallons of fuel, thus contributing to longer missions that could last up to sixteen hours. There were also fuel tanks in the bomb bay. This capability was important, especially in the Pacific Theater of operations where the bombers often had to fly over many miles of ocean in order to reach the target and then return to their bases. At the same time, this arrangement increased the chances of fires and explosions.

Consisting of about 1,250,000 parts (compared to about 7,000 for the Model T Ford), the B-24's original cost was more than $305,000, a hefty figure at a time when the average price of a new home in 1942 was less than $3,800.

Another innovation was the tricycle landing gear featured on a few of the combat aircraft produced at that time. Beginning with the Douglas A-20 Havoc, which first flew in 1938, the list also includes the B-25 Mitchell medium/light bomber, the B-26 Martin Marauder, the Douglas A-26 Invader, the Lockheed P-38 Lightning and the B-29 Superfortress, the latter of which was produced by five different companies.

This feature, on the other hand, did not help during taxiing maneuvers, which had to be accomplished by using the power of the engines on one side or the other plus the brakes. In other words, the nose wheel of this plane, unlike the front wheels of a car, could not steer it.

Carrying a normal crew complement of ten, this aircraft with a fuselage over sixty-seven feet long and eighteen feet high weighed sixty-five thousand pounds or more when loaded, and it was powered by four air-cooled Pratt & Whitney R-1830 radial engines arranged in two rows of seven cylinders each and producing 1,200 horsepower each. Later models also had General Electric B-22 turbo-compressors (superchargers) powered by the exhaust. Unless all four "fans" were turning, however, there could be problems. Unlike the B-17, which could fly on two engines, such a loss on a B-24 would create an emergency condition easily leading to a bailout.

Further, while the Flying Fortress could successfully ditch in the water or land on its belly, due to the low wing placement on the fuselage (and a number of them did just that), the high-winged fuselages of the Liberators were prone to break up in such situations; this was not exactly a confidence builder for the crews, especially when training films showed part of the fuselage breaking up after a water landing.

Liberators had ranges of 2,200 to 3,000 miles, depending on the loaded weight of the aircraft; the normal bomb carrying capacity was eight thousand pounds, or four tons. Above the dual bomb bays, by the way, was a catwalk only nine inches wide. Crewmen falling off of it—during turbulent flying conditions, for example—would not be stopped by the corrugated aluminum bomb bay "pocket" (disappearing) doors, which would not support a man's weight.

Speaking of narrow catwalks, one could say that the Liberators were not known for their roominess. Some crewmen were within arm's reach of each other, a situation that nonetheless could be an advantage during an emergency in the interest of rapid, effective communication.

Protective armament on the B-24 included a retractable belly turret (the successor to the manually operated "tunnel gun," an obsolete weapon still appearing on the B-24E model, since they were primarily used for training), an upper fuselage or top turret, a tail turret and waist gun positions on both sides. The electrically operated nose turret, which did not appear until later models, had dual .50-caliber machine guns.

This improvement may have been precipitated by a letter, dated January 12, 1943, to the Training Command (Second Air Force Training Program) from Colonel Curtis E. LeMay, who stated that "approximately 80% of all attacks are now being made from 12 o'clock." Such head-on assaults, therefore, required a lot of turret firepower aimed in that direction. In the meantime, a single machine gun was installed in the nose, and additional guns were mounted in ball sockets on both sides.

In spite of the admirable job that the Liberators did to successfully take the war to the enemy, these awkward-looking leviathans of the air that appeared to have been designed by a committee were given unflattering names, such as "Flying Brick" (or "Boxcar" or "Coffin") or the malapropism "Constipated Lumberer" instead of Consolidated Liberator.

In my humble opinion, a head-on view of the B-24 reminds me of a beautiful, graceful bird that could almost glide forever, sort of like the California condor. I must confess that while neither of them has an attractive nose, they are both built to do a job and a good one at that.

Liberators were used in both the European and Pacific Theaters of the war. After the war, some of them were used by the Indian air force for patrol purposes until the late 1960s.

Today, only about twenty intact Liberators exist, most of them in museums. Of this total, just two are flying. One is the Commemorative Air Force's *Diamond Lil*, which began life as a B-24A at Consolidated's production plant but became an LB-30 (standing for "land-based") at the end of the assembly line. Designated as a bomber/transport to be used by the British, it never made it to Europe, instead remaining here for transport and training purposes. Among the earliest Liberators produced, it is the oldest one still around and is gradually being converted to a

B-24 configuration. The Commemorative Air Force is headquartered in Midland, Texas, and has subordinate organizations around the country, most of them called "Wings," as well as a few abroad.

The other, a B-24J now called *Witchcraft* and owned by the nonprofit Collings Foundation of Stow, Massachusetts, has had various names over the years.

Seventeen other complete Liberator airframes are on static display in the United States and elsewhere. In addition, there are fifteen known partial airframes and eleven wrecked airframes in a variety of locations. And if one wants to have a really accurate count, the Liberators and their variants lying on the bottom of the various oceans, lakes and rivers around the world should be included, too.

For some years, I have also been hearing about a third Liberator, which crashed in Tequepis Canyon, opposite Cachuma Lake, sometime during the war. As the story goes, the accident occurred during a storm while the crew was on a training flight. Not having an aircraft serial number, however, I was unable to research any historical records documenting the event.

Two efforts to find the wreck site have produced no evidence thus far, but this area, which is thickly covered with chaparral (a plant community with more than eight hundred species of plants) on the northern side of the coastal mountain range, is an extreme challenge to traverse by foot, unless a trail or road has been built…or you are a quail or a rabbit. Even though much of this was brush burned during the Refugio Fire of 1955, thus exposing the terrain and perhaps remnants of the wreck supposedly there, chaparral recovers fast, as I have learned from volunteer trail work for the forest service.

A Bomber Crash Behind the Coastal Mountain Range

The research project began in late 1991, about a decade after a friend, Tom Butera, informed me about a Liberator wreck site behind our coastal mountains. I began by writing a letter, on behalf of the now defunct Goleta/Santa Barbara Air Heritage Museum, to the Santa Barbara district ranger of the Los Padres National Forest about the possibilities of acquiring relics from the wreck site for the purposes of their preservation and public display as a part of our local aviation heritage. I was hoping that being a member of this museum and using its letterhead stationery would enhance my credentials in this crusade. I am not sure if it ever did, but in a few cases, the customary fees of various federal government entities were waived, supposedly because I was acting on behalf of this organization.

Ranger Pontes's response stated:

> *This letter is to confirm for you that we are interested in assisting you preserve this WW-II aircraft locally. The final approval process, however, will take a little longer than what you appeared to anticipate in your letter. The Forest Service has a legal process to complete whenever there is a project involving a potentially historic site, including aircraft wrecks. In essence the aircraft needs to be inventoried (physical description of site and remains as well as documentary research) and evaluated for historic significance. Los Padres NF has no expertise in historic aircraft. The process will only move along if the Air Heritage Museum can provide expertise and assistance for the inventory and evaluation work. Steve [Horne] understands from your recent conversation that the Air Heritage Museum or members of*

TIGHAR might be able to do this work on a volunteer basis. When the work is completed and determined adequate, the Forest will have to consult with the State Historic Preservation Office and the Advisory Council on Historic Preservation.

Fortunately, this position was not in conflict with the air force view contained in a letter I received about fifteen months later. In it, Jeff D. Hallett (Disposal Policy, Directorate of Logistics, Headquarters Air Force Materiel Command at Wright-Patterson Air Force Base in Ohio) quoted Air Force Regulation 126-7, Historic Preservation, dated August 28, 1987, which noted:

Aircraft that crashed before 19 November 1961, when a fire destroyed the pertinent AF records, and that remain wholly or partially unrecovered [sic]*, are considered formally abandoned. The Air Force neither maintains title to, nor has property interest in these aircraft. The authority for access to, and recovery of these aircraft, as well as liability for damages associated with their recovery, are matters to be resolved between persons seeking recovery and landowners of the wreckage site.*

In alignment with this position is a letter, dated September 10, 1992, from Richard E. Gillespie, executive director of the International Group for Historic Aircraft Recovery (TIGHAR), in which he stated, in part:

For several years the Air Force has claimed to have abandoned its aircraft lost before 1961. Technically a federal agency can not [sic] *abandon property but, from a practical standpoint, if it's an old USAAF airplane, you won't get any grief from the Air Force. If, by any chance, it's a U.S. Navy PB4Y then you have a very different situation and a high probability that the Navy will confiscate anything you recover.*

Ranger Pontes's letter led to contact with the national forest archaeologist, Steven Horne, and TIGHAR, based in Wilmington, Delaware, in order to determine what steps could legally be taken to accomplish the stated objective. Even though the wreck had been there for nearly half a century, someone still owned it, and guidance would have to be obtained, according to the district ranger, from organizations such as the California Historic Preservation Office and the Advisory Council on Historic Preservation.

Steve, by the way, searched through the Los Padres National Forest record files and produced a copy of the Individual Fire Report, which was very helpful in piecing together this story. I also visited the Santa Barbara Public Library and looked through the microfilm files to see if there were any articles about this event in the *Santa Barbara News-Press*. I was fortunate to find three, all published within about a week.

On Monday, July 5, 1943, the *Santa Barbara News-Press* reported the crash on its front page. The article noted that eight members of the ten-man crew jumped from the bomber and landed on forestland north of the city. In the meantime, the aircraft, with no one aboard, continued to fly over the coastal mountain range and crashed in a canyon on the other side after circling a lookout twice. The article further stated that the survivors were taken to Hoff Hospital and treated for cuts and bruises.

A follow-up article the next day, also on the front page, reported that the search was continuing for the two crew members who had bailed out over the water about one hundred miles west of Santa Barbara. Officials at the Salinas Army Air Base reportedly advised that the names of the other eight crew members would not be released "as long as the search for the other two was underway."

A week later, after the search ended, the names of these missing crew members were published in an article that appeared on page B-1. This report did not, however, note that two or three days after the bailout, the navigator and bombardier's parachutes, according to a surviving crew member, were found near the shoreline north of Santa Barbara, possibly in the Goleta or Elwood area.

In the meantime, a short article entitled "10 Parachute as Plane Crashes; 2 Men Missing" appeared in an unknown newspaper. The dateline is "SANTA BARBARA, July 5 (INS)," and the second paragraphs reads, "It was reported, however, that two men—possibly the missing airmen—had been sighted on a raft near Cape [Point] Sal and that a Naval vessel had gone to the scene." If such an event did occur, all that is known for sure is that the missing bombardier and navigator were not on that raft.

On Wednesday, July 14, the following article, entitled "Hunt Ends for Remsen Air Officer" appeared in the *Utica (NY) Observer Dispatch*: "Search for Lt. Robert Prosser, Remsen, missing in a plane lost off the Santa Barbara coast, has been abandoned, as Henry Prosser, the air officer's father has been informed in a wire from the commanding officer at the Santa Barbara Air Base."

Mr. Prosser first learned of his son's disappearance the previous week in a brief message. The second message, received Monday, read:

Search for Lt. Robert H. Prosser has been abandoned. Entire area by route of aircraft was searched for four days by aircraft by this group and naval vessels and blimp.

Lt. Prosser's parachute was found floating in the ocean off the coast of Santa Barbara. Lt. Prosser was not found. Any reports concerning the accident will be investigated by this headquarters and you will be informed of such developments immediately.

He was expected home that week on a ten-day furlough.

While these airmen may possibly have landed safely in the water and released their harnesses, they could have drowned due to the weight of their flight clothing—which could have thwarted their efforts to remain afloat—and the fact that the flotation equipment used for such occasions was still on the plane. In addition, a water temperature of about sixty degrees could eventually have led to hypothermia and death. It is also possible that, due to the lack of light, they misjudged their distance from the water and, fearing entanglement in their parachute lines upon landing, released the harnesses too soon and fell into the water from too great a height.

In spite of the termination of the search, the names of the eight crewmen who successfully bailed out were not mentioned in the third *Santa Barbara News-Press* article cited earlier.

Lieutenant Robert H. Prosser, the bombardier aboard the *Hat in the Ring* (*Eddie Rickenbacker*), B-24E, 42-7011, bailed out over the ocean before the aircraft reached the Santa Barbara coast during a training flight originating at the Salinas Army Air Field. While his parachute, as well as the one used by navigator Lieutenant Peter J. Dannhardt, was found near Goleta two or three days later, neither of their bodies was ever recovered. This photo is probably a professionally taken portrait. Photographer unknown.

A Chain of Tragedies across Air, Land and Sea

While this instance was not the only time that someone had to bail out of an airplane in an emergency situation, it undoubtedly holds the record for the number of crewman, ten of them in this case, doing so at about the same time.

The plane crash—not "off the coast," as stated in the article quoted earlier—was observed by two forest service lookout personnel who were either awake or awakened when the approaching crewless aircraft made at least a semicircle around the tower, thus being a matter of great concern to them, before slamming into a chaparral-covered slope about a mile away at an elevation of 2,500 feet. The impact fragmented most of the major components of the bomber and scattered numerous parts over a wide area in the canyon. Some of them might have even been launched over a nearby ridge and into an adjacent canyon.

While the names of the two people in the lookout on Camuesa Peak (elevation 3,170 feet) have been lost in the winds of history, I did learn something about their experience from Raymond W. Richart, a forest service radio technician and communications officer who visited the site shortly afterward. During the war, he assisted in the installation and maintenance of aircraft warning stations (AWS) on higher peaks overlooking the California coast. He worked for the forest service between 1916 and his retirement in 1950. It therefore appears that this incident may have been, in a sense, the largest "Fourth of July fireworks display" in the history of Santa Barbara County, but only two people saw it.

About a minute later, at 2:15 a.m., one of them reported the crash by telephone, and a seven-man fire suppression crew was dispatched from the Los Prietos Ranger Station, which was about twelve miles away. Nearly half of this distance was over the narrow, winding, uphill Camuesa Road. Arriving about an hour later, the crew members still had to walk half a mile to reach the crash site.

The movement of the resulting fire was described as "creeping," and less than an acre burned, most of it occurring before the fire crew arrived. Fortunately, there was only a two-mile-per-hour breeze, and the humidity level at that time was probably high enough to discourage the fire from moving very fast. Mop-up operations were completed by 7:00 a.m.

The forest service's Individual Fire Report, from which the previous information was taken, includes the name of the boss of the fire fighters. Eighteen years later, I interviewed this man, Erwin Lyda, on behalf of the Order of the Arrow, a Boy Scouts of America honor camping society that, among other projects, promotes camping among scout units and others.

To help meet this objective, I was gathering some historical information about the backcountry from retired forest service employees to include in a forthcoming camping guide. I did not realize until twenty years later, when I first learned about the Liberator wreck site, that this man would have been a valuable source of information for that project, too. But when it started, ten years after that, time had run out because he had joined the great majority "on the other side of the hedge."

That only a small area burned is remarkable, however, for two reasons. First, the explosion and resulting fire was caused by a four-engine bomber that still had some fuel aboard plus a load of ordnance, including, according to the accident report, twenty bombs and 1,200 rounds of .50-caliber machine gun ammunition. (Gunner Gail Vanlandingham stated that there were 3,000 rounds of this ammunition in groups of 600 rounds each and that the bombs were practice bombs.) Heat from the explosion and fire ignited them and added to the incendiary results.

Second, the primary chaparral plant in this area was chamise, which is also called "greasewood." This type of vegetation does not merely burn; it explodes and helps fires to spread faster. At the same time, chamise is among those plants that regenerate first, often within a few weeks, even though the rainy season may still be months away. Like other plants in the chaparral community, it has a substantial root system beneath the surface of the ground and is therefore protected from the heat of a fire.

If one wonders why live ammunition, including bombs, was carried aboard on training flights, the crew was prepared to attack targets of opportunity if the occasion arose. In the case of the California coastal area, one must remember that Japanese I-class submarines (more than 300 feet long) torpedoed five ships off the California coast during the latter part of December 1941. These consisted of two freighters and three tankers, including the SS *Montebello*, a 440-foot-long tanker carrying more than 3 million gallons of crude oil and a 100,000 gallons of fuel oil, which was sunk only six miles off the coast of Cambria, not far from the Hearst Castle.

An interesting sidenote about the *Montebello* is that just before it was scheduled to leave the port, the captain learned that a Japanese submarine had been seen in the area. With concerns about the safety of his crew and ship, he decided not to sail and was thereafter obliged to resign his position and leave the ship. The first mate then assumed command of the vessel, which began its voyage a short time later, only to be torpedoed and sunk by the *I-21* several hours later. The thirty-eight crew members escaped in lifeboats, although they were briefly subjected to the submarine's deck gun firing before it submerged to avoid being seen by patrolling aircraft. The incident, though reported, was not publicized due to a fear that it would cause panic among California's coastal populations.

Two months later, however, another event occurred, and there was no way to stop the publicity on this one. On February 23, 1942, the Ellwood oil field near Goleta was shelled by the deck gun of a Japanese submarine identified as the *I-17*. While the physical damage was minimal, not amounting to more than about $500, the psychological repercussions among those living anywhere near the coast were enormous.

A dramatic but questionable explanation of this event is a local story that has been making the rounds for years. The submarine's commander, Kozo Nishino, had reportedly been an oil tanker captain before the war, and during one particular visit to the Ellwood field to take a load of crude oil destined for Japan, he fell into a cactus patch while trying to photograph it; due to the resulting embarrassment in front of his crew, he vowed revenge, and his subsequent command of a submarine was apparently a convenient way to do it.

At any rate, the incident was a very scary moment in our local history, and it was probably the best time to purchase real estate in Hope Ranch, an affluent residential area west of Santa Barbara.

About eight weeks later, we returned the favor when Colonel Jimmy Doolittle and a group of volunteers took off from an aircraft carrier in 16 B-25 medium bombers to drop some ordnance over Japan, thought to be an impenetrable fortress at that time.

Returning to the latter-day investigation, when I gathered the information just described, the next step was to request a special use permit from the forest service. This would allow us to inventory the site and create a topographic map on which the items would be numbered, identified (whenever possible) and located. The services of a forest service land surveyor were also secured to help prepare a map of the wreck site.

Returning to the site on a subsequent visit, however, proved to be a bit of a challenge, but one of the accompanying rangers, John Bridgwater, had a botanical background, and he noted that some of the vegetation in one of the canyons was different than what surrounded it. Instead of the dominant chamise, which covered the hillside before the fire, there were now other members of the chaparral family, including various types of ceanothus and sage, plus yerba santa, buckwheat and a variety of grasses. Once dominant vegetation burned, competing plants quickly established themselves and thus later provided clues to the crash site's location.

Searching for the Official Records

The next move was to contact an organization that could supply us with information, official and otherwise, about the wreck. Letters were sent to the USAF Historical Research Center at Maxwell Air Force Base in Alabama; the Military Reference Branch of the National Archive of the United States in Washington, D.C.; the National Air and Space Museum Library and Archives of the Smithsonian Institution in Washington, D.C.; the USAF Museum at Wright-Patterson Air Force Base in Ohio; and the Fred E. Weisbrod/International B-24 Memorial Museum in Pueblo, Colorado.

Inquiries were also sent to the *Veterans of Foreign Wars* magazine, the *Air Force* magazine and the *American Legion* magazine in search of survivors or relatives of survivors who could possibly provide more details, especially the personal experiences, about these events.

In addition, a correspondence was established with the Thirty-fourth Bomb Group Association and the International B-24 Liberator Club to see if any of their members belonged to the *Hat in the Ring* aircrew or knew, or knew of, any of the men who did.

The first significant breakthrough occurred in early 1994 when I received a copy of the "Report of Aircraft Accident," or rather the "releasable portions," from the Air Force Safety Agency at Kirtland Air Force Base in New Mexico. The reasons why the entire report was not released to me were as follows:

1. Release of this information would have a stifling effect on the free and frank expression of ideas and opinions of Air Force officials. 2. In order to promote full disclosure, witnesses are promised by the mishap investigation board that their testimony will be used solely for mishap prevention and for no other purpose. This promise of confidentiality is made in order to encourage witnesses to disclose to the investigating board everything they know about the mishap even though the statements they make may be against their personal interest or possibly incriminating.

I was also informed that I could appeal this decision by writing to the secretary of the air force within sixty calendar days and stating my reasons for reconsideration. I did so and explained:

Our museum is not seeking information that would be critical of, or possibly incriminate, witnesses who gave testimony before the investigating board. We are interested, however, in knowing the cause or causes of what appears to be the largest aircraft accident in the history of Santa Barbara County. We are aware of three reports that offer varying explanations of what happened.

The apparent persuasiveness of this letter, as well as a little patience, paid off when I received the complete copy of the accident report nearly two years later. Finally, here was a document that not only identified the crew members aboard the aircraft, as well as some other pertinent facts, but also provided the statements submitted by surviving crew members, as well the findings of the accident investigation board.

Seeking Surviving Crew Members

The next step was to attempt to locate any of the original crew members who were still alive nearly half a century later. This was a difficult task, but I wanted to learn, if possible, what these men did during the rest of the war. In spite of their trials and tribulations, they were gaining experience as a bomber crew, and bomber crews were in high demand.

After sending advertisements to the three magazines in an attempt to locate living survivors, I received one response from a Herkimer, New York man who stated that the missing navigator, Lieutenant Robert H. Prosser, was his grandmother's nephew. He then asked why I was looking for survivors. Replying to his letter, I explained that we were "compiling a history of this event which is an important chapter in the aviation history of our area." I further stated that if he had any information that would help us in our efforts, his assistance would be appreciated. I never heard from him again.

On the other hand, a representative of the Thirty-fourth Bomb Group Association provided me with some information about the assistant radio operator, George C. Belitskus. His son, George C. Belitskus Jr., happened to be a member of the Eighth Air Force Historical Society, and his name was spotted on a membership roster by the Thirty-fourth Bomb Group Association representative, Harold E. Province, who was also an Eighth Air Force Historical Society contact.

George Jr. later provided some copies of materials relating to his late father's USAAF career. These included the cover of a receivers laboratory manual; a radio operators and mechanics course diploma dated February

27, 1943, from the Army Air Forces Technical School at Sioux Falls Field, South Dakota; a Biggs Field (also known as Biggs Army Airfield, Texas) transient aircraft crew pass; a graduation picture; and a poem he probably wrote to his wife, or future wife. It reads:

> *Oh! The nights are long & Dreary,*
> *Especially when we are studing* [sic] *Theory—*
> *We come from Code to this humble adobe.*
> *And there we stay till its time to hit the hay.*
> *The only thing that makes it bearable is*
> *my dreams of you my adorable* [illegible].
> *When the war is done, oh wont* [sic] *we have fun.*
> *So my dear, be of good cheer and I hope to*
> *be there within a year?*

While a namesake situation helped me to obtain information about this crew member, I still had not, at this point, been able to contact one who was still alive.

Finding the Needle in the Haystack

My next step was to attempt a contact through the Veterans Administration Records Processing Center in St. Louis, Missouri. After submitting the names of the seven crew members not accounted for, I was subsequently informed that there were claim numbers for four of them and that if I wished to have letters forwarded to them, "they should be submitted…using the file number referenced in an unsealed envelope with NO return address and bearing sufficient postage to cover mailing cost. You may include your address in your letters. We can offer no assurance that the veterans will either receive or respond to your correspondence."

I was also advised that two of the crew members—Thorel T. Johnson (the pilot) and Braydon L. Hassinger (the assistant engineer)—were both deceased and that no VA records could be found for Gail Vanlandingham, with the explanation, "It is possible that we would be unable to identify records for this veteran if she never applied for Veterans Administration benefits." If Gail, in this case, turned out to be a "she," it would have undoubtedly been the only instance during the war that a female was a member of any combat air crew.

Of the four letters sent by the VA, all were returned by the post office as undeliverable. In the case of copilot George White, the last address in the VA files was dated June 1947. At this point, I decided to utilize an address search directory on the Internet in order to find any crew members who might still be alive. In four of the cases, however, either the names were not listed or there were hundreds of them with fairly common names. Such was the case with George White.

The fifth case, however, involved a very unusual name, Gail Vanlandingham. The directory I used had about 90 million names and addresses and listed only one person with this name. Thus, in 1996, five years after I began gathering information about this Liberator wreck site, I sent a letter to Mr. Vanlandingham in Issaquah, Washington, and asked, "Were you a crew member of a B-24 Liberator which crashed in our back country in July, 1943?"

Responding to my letter five days later, he replied, "Yes I was a member of the B-24 Liberator that crashed in the area you spoke of." The door to the next level of this project had just opened.

This response presented the opportunity to learn what happened to the surviving crew members beyond what the accident report tells us. In other words, how did these men spend the rest of the war? Correspondence with Gail, an armor gunner who flew in both the top turret and waist gunner positions, led to contact with the only other crew member still alive, John Wedesky, the first radio operator, who lived in Janesville, Wisconsin.

Communication with both of these men was conducted by mail and telephone calls. In addition, they recorded their experiences on audio cassette tapes (on behalf of the Commemorative Air Force Oral History Program, as well as this project), which I then transcribed into hard copies by using only a standard tape recorder, which, unlike a transcription machine, is not designed for constant starting and stopping in order to write what was said. These hard copies were then mailed to them to proofread because I wanted to make sure that the stories, as they recalled them, were as accurate as possible.

The resulting stories provided by Gail and John revealed information not available in any of the documents collected up to that time. The story of this crew begins at a time when such groups were assembled and trained at combat training centers throughout the country in order to meet the urgent demands for the war raging overseas in both the European and the Pacific Theaters of operations. One of these training centers was the Salinas Army Air Base near Salinas, California. Under the command of the Thirty-fourth Bombardment Group of the Second Air Force, this facility's mission was to rapidly and extensively train aircrews so that each member became proficient in his particular specialty, whether it was as a pilot, navigator, bombardier, gunner or other.

In order to accomplish this goal, a lot of flying at any time of the day or night would be necessary. And until the crew became experienced, the possibilities of mistakes and accidents were always higher. Now that the crew members were all on permanent flying status, there is a record of at least one of them purchasing a $12,000.00 life insurance policy, with $6.60 monthly premiums. Perhaps all of them did this. I recall doing the same at the beginning of my brief air force flight training experience nineteen years later.

Salinas Army Air Base was a temporary home for the Thirty-fourth Bombardment Group, however. While the fog here could be a problem for any aircraft activity, the organization's "permanent" home at the Army Air Field in Blythe, California, presented some significant challenges due to the hot weather. After spending several weeks in Tucson, Arizona, for training, the crew left on May 15, 1943, and headed for Blythe, California.

As Gail Vanlandingham observed, "Blythe looked nice from the sky but wasn't a very nice field." Here, according to the late Ray Summa, who was stationed at Blythe during that period, "the asphalt on the runways was rolling up around the tires of the aircraft...Some of the A/C mechanics kept a pail of kerosene handy in order to cool off the metal wrenches they were using on the A/C...most of the A/C maintenance was accomplished at night after it had cooled down a little."

Further, without shelter in this desert location, summer temperatures sometimes reached 160 degrees inside the planes and on the tarmac. And if the working conditions were not bad enough, add to that the challenges of basic living conditions in barracks, which, of course, had no air conditioning. Things were apparently so bad that one unsubstantiated rumor revealed that the chaplain "went over the hill" before April Fools' Day in 1942. Interesting timing.

These "warm" circumstances led to the unit's temporary relocation. Arriving in Salinas on June 1, the men were scheduled to spend about two months in the cool lettuce producing climate not far from the coast. Here, as well as at other locations, the living experience was enhanced, at least for the married members of the crew. For example, Estel Johnson and Elizabeth White, wives of the pilot and copilot, respectively, lived with their husbands at a motel called the Rainbow, which was located about one mile south of that city.

But the problems did not end in a more comfortable climate. It was during a short period in 1943 when a number of Liberators from the Thirty-fourth Bombardment Group crashed in California with a large loss of airmen, a phenomenon fairly typical (and tragic) in training environments. Some of the events surrounding two of these accidents are related, and it can therefore be said that the misfortunes experienced on one of these aircraft indirectly led to a catastrophe involving the other.

The Ten-Hour Flight that Ended with an Unscheduled Stop

On the evening of July 3, 1943, crew no. 13, of the 391st Bomb Squadron (Heavy), 34th Bombardment Group (Heavy) and 1st Bomber Command of the Second Air Force (a training organization), boarded its B-24E (a relatively rare model, as only 801 of them were manufactured; 490 of them, including this one, were built by the Ford Motor Company), serial no. 42-7011, at the Salinas Army Air Base in California. After checking on the condition of the aircraft, the crew determined that it was ready to fly. Its load included 2,300 gallons of aviation gas and a full load of twenty bombs, plus ammunition for the .50-caliber machine guns.

Like other combat aircraft of the period, it sported a nose art cartoon showing Eddie Rickenbacker, with his name above, throwing a hat into a ring. Also shown were the last three digits of the aircraft's serial number. This illustration was inspired by the Ninety-fourth Aero Pursuit Squadron, a pioneer World War I flight organization, which was also called the "Hat in the Ring" squadron. Its best-known member was Captain Edward V. Rickenbacker (1890–1973), who fought in more than 130 air battles and shot down twenty-six enemy planes. This record achievement earned him the title "American Ace of Aces." In addition to being awarded the Congressional Medal of Honor, he was a race car driver and an automotive designer; an automobile bearing his name was manufactured in Detroit, Michigan, between 1922 and 1928. He also participated in World War II and later became a longtime president of Eastern Airlines.

Photographs of this particular aircraft include one on the ground, with all four engines running. The hangar in the background suggests that this picture

B-24E, 42-7011, the *Hat in the Ring*. The hangar in the background suggests that this photo may have been taken at Ford's Willow Run manufacturing plant near Detroit, Michigan. Photographer unknown.

may have been taken where the plane was manufactured, Ford's Willow Run plant near Detroit, Michigan. Another one shows Eddie Rickenbacker himself standing near the nose art created in his honor, plus two close-ups of the cartoon.

While this design, plus the ones on other bombers flown by this crew, would undoubtedly not be considered "racy" by anyone's standards, many expressions of such illustrations on World War II aircraft were. Although images of young, scantily clad women in a variety of seductive poses might have been considered pornographic by some observers, there is much more to this medium created so far away from the homes of these airmen.

As Karra O'Connell described in a Commemorative Air Force publication article entitled "World War II: The Golden Age of Nose Art," this type of graphic portrayal "was the fusion of the self-expression of fighting men and the mass-produced weapons of war that created such dynamic examples of American folk art."

The medium was further explained by Captain Stanley Washburn, who declared in a 1944 *Stars and Stripes* article that it "represents the very essence and spirit of the young, hell-bent-for-election American crews who fly and fight [in] these ships and endow them with their own personalities." He also added Nobel Prize–winning author John Steinbeck's view that it was "illustrated literature...the finest writing to come out of the war."

While the combat aircraft produced during that era may have been virtually identical upon leaving the assembly lines, it was the nose art that gave them their own individual identities, even on the mundane assignments, such as the one that follows as we continue the uneventful turned eventful story of the *Hat in the Ring*'s training flight on July 3, 1943.

Their assigned mission that evening was an over-water nighttime navigation mission that was expected to last for ten hours. After setting the superchargers and checking the magnetos, the pilot taxied the aircraft

A Chain of Tragedies across Air, Land and Sea

This additional nose art on B-24, 42-7011, identifies the aircraft as the *Eddie Rickenbacker*, even though at least one crew member referred to it as the *Hat in the Ring*. This photograph may have been taken at the Willow Run (Michigan) manufacturing plant. Photographer unknown.

More nose art on the *Hat in the Ring* (*Eddie Rickenbacker*). This symbol was used by the Ninety-fourth Aero Pursuit Squadron during World War I. Its best-known member was Captain Edward V. Rickenbacker, who shot down twenty-six enemy planes and became known as the "American Aces of Aces." The image was probably taken for publicity purposes. Photographer unknown.

for the scheduled takeoff at 7:00 p.m., climbed to an altitude of ten thousand feet and then began a one-thousand-mile flight in accordance with headings provided by the navigator. The plan called for flying out over the ocean for four hundred miles and then heading inland to the Bakersfield Army Air Field, now the Bakersfield Municipal Airport.

Since such flights had few geographical checkpoints for the navigator, he was obliged to use a sextant (literally meaning "one-sixth of a circle"), an astronomical instrument invented in the 1700s and employed to measure angular distances of celestial bodies (such as the sun, moon and the North Star, or Polaris). By getting "fixes" on the stars through a transparent dome built into the fuselage just above the forward crew compartment in the nose of the aircraft, he could then determine the position and direction of the aircraft. Computing wind drift was another important and necessary skill of the navigator.

This flight, then, was primarily an exercise for the navigator, although it seems likely that the pilots, too, would benefit from accumulating nighttime flying hours. The other crew members, however, didn't have much to do except, perhaps, drink coffee of less than the best quality. The gunners would probably have no targets to shoot at, nor would the bombardier likely have targets to bomb.

The details of the events that occurred later on this flight, however, are incomplete in terms of exactly what happened and when it happened. According to the Report of Aircraft Accident, the original AAF Form No. 1—Flight Report Operations and AAF Form No. 1A—Flight Report Engine rin-(?) were lost in the crash. The accident report does, however, include statements by the pilot, copilot and first engineer plus the findings of a board of inquiry that was convened after the crash. In addition, observations shared with me by the two living survivors of this accident, and/or their family members, helped to piece together what probably happened until the aircraft crashed in Camuesa Canyon behind Santa Barbara.

The pilot's explanation noted that the gas consumption was higher than expected and that their route should be changed to fly over Point Arguello and then land in Bakersfield. When the aircraft was about one hour and twenty minutes away from Point Arguello, however, the no. 1 engine quit and never ran again despite several attempts to start it.

Then the no. 2 engine began "acting up," and the pilot anticipated that it, too, would quit before the plane was over land. At this time, he ordered the crew to prepare to bail out. When the navigator "sighted Pt. Arguello and the light line," the no. 2 engine quit as the aircraft passed the second beacon. It was apparently at this point, when the airspeed "dropped off," according to the pilot's statement in the Report of Aircraft Accident, that the navigator and bombardier bailed out through the nose wheel well. This was at a time when the aircraft was still over the water, and both of them were probably aware of this fact.

As one experienced former air force pilot observed:

I would assume the navigator thought he had a good fix/position otherwise why leave the aircraft overwater, especially unchallenged. Secondly, from my time flying in the Air Force, unless the aircraft is out of control or coming apart, or pilots incapacitated (which wasn't the case here), there are orders to prepare to bailout and then the command to do so either by voice or bell, I suppose, in the B-24.

While there was no order to actually jump (instead, to *prepare* to do so), their hasty departure may have been encouraged by not only what was (or was not) going on with the engines but also by what happened in the cockpit, when, according to the armor gunner, the pilot left his seat to use the pilot-to-ground radio.

The copilot, now flying the aircraft, inexplicably raised the nose, perhaps in an attempt to gain altitude. The result, however, was a decrease of airspeed and a loss of about two thousand feet of altitude during a period of three or four minutes.

In the meantime, the no. 2 engine was successfully restarted, but it only ran for a few minutes before quitting again. This event apparently happened more than once. In addition, 275 gallons of fuel were lost from the no. 1 tank "while the engine was cut off and the [fuel] valve closed." Just before the aircraft arrived at the coast, the fuel gauges showed that 1,200 gallons of fuel were left on board, but after Santa Barbara was circled a few times, only one hundred gallons remained, at least according to the gauges that, reportedly, were known to be accurate until the tanks were almost empty.

Bailout!

While several attempts were made to establish radio contact with ground stations, including the base, there were no responses. Both the transmitters and receivers were no longer functioning for some reason, and the radio direction finder was of no help either.

After the Liberator was guided in a direction inland from Santa Barbara, the pilot and aircraft commander, Lieutenant Johnson, ordered the remaining members of the crew to bail out. As he later stated in the accident report, "The ship hit a mountain and burned." In this report, prepared after the accident, the copilot's statement, very similar to the pilot's, indicated that the first sign of trouble occurred some time after the mission began. This was when "the ship seemed a bit sluggish" and the "airspeed was only 150–155 M.P.H." Very soon thereafter, the first engineer advised that fuel consumption was much higher than normal. It is possible that offshore headwinds could have been a factor here.

The engineer's statement was also very much like these, but the departure of the navigator and the bombardier was explained by the words, "On some misunderstanding of orders, we lost the Navigator and Bombardier." Further, while he provided a more detailed account about the fuel situation, as would be expected of an engineer, the mystery of the disappearing (and reappearing) fuel continued without explanation:

> *When I shut the fuel valve "off" on No. 1 Engine, it had 375 gallons of gas in the tank. When the fuel ran considerably low in the other three tanks, I switched the No. 1 valve to the other tanks, and at that time I noticed there*

was [sic] *only 100 gallons on the whole plane (according to the gauges).
Just before we hit the Coast, there was* [sic] *1200 gallons on board, and
after circling Santa Barbara I looked again and found that 100 gallons
was all that remained. There was* [sic] *no leaks on the inner wing or in the
fuel lines because the Assistant and I checked that after noticing the large
consumption of fuel.*

Even though the conclusions of both the pilot's and first engineer's
statement are the same, there were nevertheless a few discrepancies in their
reports. First, the pilot advised a loss of 275 gallons of gas from the no. 1
tank. The engineer, on the other hand, mentioned 375 gallons remaining
in this tank (typographical error?) and that he transferred the fuel from this
location to the remaining three tanks.

Second, after completing this transfer, he noticed that the gauges showed
only 100 gallons of gas on the entire aircraft. This figure then somehow
increased to 1,200 gallons (more than half of the amount of fuel on board
at the beginning of the flight in Salinas) just before arriving over the coast
and then dropped to 100 gallons again after the plane circled Santa Barbara
several times.

Armor gunner Gail Vanlandingham's recollection, given to me fifty-four
years after the accident, advised that the mission was uneventful until the
aircraft had flown four hundred miles over water and then turned to head
toward Bakersfield, where it would land. After making the turn, the no. 1
engine stopped; here, the aircraft was about two hundred miles from shore.
With the propeller feathered, the plane continued flying for about half an
hour on three engines until the no. 2 engine also quit about one hundred
miles from shore.

Shortly before reaching shore, the no. 3 engine reportedly failed. At this point,
the aircraft suddenly went into a dive, and the bombardier and the navigator,
whose stations were in the nose, bailed out through the nose wheel well. They
apparently did this before there was any order to prepare to bail out because
they did not respond to a crew report (role call).

The remainder of the crew stayed with the aircraft for a few more minutes
and continued flying down the coast. They then saw what appeared to be
Santa Barbara, which, by the lights, looked like a town of about five hundred
people, but they were not sure since the navigator was no longer aboard.
The whole coast was blacked out because the aircraft came in where it was
not supposed to be. At this point, the decision was made to bail out since
they knew that there were nearby mountains higher than they were.

Further, in view of both engines on the port (left) side of the aircraft shutting down, according to all three statements in the accident report, it was much more difficult to control the bomber. Add to this predicament another dead engine on the starboard (right) side, and all that remained was an underpowered motorized glider that was not gliding very well.

In addition, the darkness at that time, about two o'clock in the morning, complicated matters even more. Never having jumped before, the remaining eight crewmen were understandably apprehensive about bailing out, especially under these conditions.

As Gail Vanlandingham explained in a letter many years later, "No one in the aft section wanted to be the first to jump. This was our first jump. I ask[ed] them if I jumped would they follow me, they said yes. I jumped into the night."

All of them successfully parachuted from the ailing aircraft as it flew over the San Marcos Pass area. Even though by this time there was only one engine still running, when Gail bailed out, it was probably then able to stay aloft a little longer with nearly a ton of its human cargo no longer aboard. As he later wrote, however, "The airplane just wouldn't maintain altitude on one engine."

The following reports, given more than half a century after this incident occurred, were provided by the last two surviving crew members. While radio operator John Wedesky recalled seeing the ocean during the bailout, Gail Vanlandingham remembered that it was a dark and moonless night. Hence, not only could he not see the ground, he could not gauge his distance from it either. With his parachute continuously oscillating on the way down, he ended up on a rock and was knocked unconscious. Upon regaining consciousness, he discovered a knot on the side of his head.

At this point, he took about three steps, "stepped into air," slid down a steep embankment that seemed like forty or fifty feet and stopped on what appeared to be a ledge. Instead of standing up, for fear of falling over the "ledge," he felt around with his hands, and in the process, he noticed a white line. Concluding that he was in the middle of a road (the San Marcos Pass Road, now known as State Route 154), he waited to hail a passing car, of which there were sure to be few so early in the morning. When one finally did approach, it refused to stop. Perhaps the occupants were scared because there was a war on, and Gail, standing there in a high-altitude flying suit, may have looked like the enemy or perhaps even an extraterrestrial invader.

Several more cars passed by, but they did not stop either. Finally, when one with flashing red lights approached, he was determined to stop it by standing in the middle of the road. It did, but the occupants, sheriff's deputies, emerged from the car with their guns drawn. After he assured them that he was an American, they explained that they had received a radio report about an airplane crash in the mountains. They remained in the area until daylight and spent the time looking for the other crew members. During this period, the battery in the patrol car was almost drained because of the time spent using the radio.

The deputies' concerns about Gail's identity in this instance are understandable. Just eighteen months beforehand, a Japanese submarine well over three hundred feet long (in other words, longer than a football field) had surfaced near Goleta, about a mile offshore, and lobbed about twenty-five shells from its 5½-inch deck gun at the Ellwood oil field. The physical damage caused by the attack amounted to only about $500, but the psychological blow it delivered to the nation was devastating. This attack, incidentally, was the first enemy naval bombardment of the United States mainland since the War of 1812.

Second engineer and ball turret gunner Staff Sergeant Braydon Hassinger apparently joined this group at some point, too, since according to his hometown newspaper, he "landed a few yards off a highway and was picked up by patrolmen." All of them remained in the area until daylight and spent the time looking for the other crew members.

Another crewman, pilot Thorel "Skip" (perhaps an abbreviated name for skipper of the aircraft?) Johnson, who was the last one to leave the stricken aircraft, may have seen it crash in Camuesa (a probable corruption of the Spanish term *gamuza*, which means "chamois") Canyon when he bailed out on the Santa Ynez Valley side of the coast range. At the end of his descent, however, he had the misfortune of landing in a tall tree on a steep hillside. Attempting to climb down in the dark, he was unable to see the ground and consequently decided to return to the point from where he started and wait for daylight.

After successfully "completing his descent" when there was enough light to see, he then walked down a long dirt road with switchbacks. Not wanting to miss a chance to get a ride if a car appeared, he did not wish to cut any of these switchbacks. Once he reached the bottom, he discovered a locked gate and learned that the road was closed for the duration of the war. The route he walked is probably the Camuesa Road, which ends (or begins) at the locked gate at Upper Oso Campground. Closed to the public during World War II, it is still largely inaccessible except for motorcycles and quadricycles.

In the meantime, radio operator John Wedesky landed near a road. Remaining there until it was light enough to see, he and some of the other crewmen, including copilot George White, walked down a road to the home of a civilian doctor, who provided them with a breakfast of orange juice and eggs until they could get a ride into Santa Barbara. I suppose one could say they literally "dropped in for breakfast."

Not remembering their host's name, which is certainly understandable after over fifty years, they apparently encountered one of two, or possibly more, doctors living in the vicinity. One possibility long considered was Dr. Charles Jobbins, a Santa Barbara physician whose California bungalow-style home, destroyed in the Painted Cave Fire of 1990, was located just off the San Marcos Pass Road (now also designated as State Highway 154) just above the San Antonio Creek bridge.

A check through some Santa Barbara city directories, however, indicated that the Jobbins family lived at 1335 Dover Road, which is located on the Riviera section of the city, and did not move to their San Marcos Pass Road address, called Rancho El Gato, until 1945, two years after the bailout.

There was, however, another civilian doctor who lived just east of the San Marcos Pass Road. Dr. Horace Pierce and his family had an avocado and lemon ranch in this area, and he could possibly have been the host on this occasion. The 1941 Santa Barbara City Directory lists his residence as Vista del Mundo (Spanish for "view of the world") Ranch, which in 2011 was on the real estate market as a 1,500-acre parcel. Since ranches generally have roads, one of them could have been used by these crew members to find the house. Unfortunately, no relatives, who could possibly corroborate this story, have been located.

That Dr. Pierce lived on this property in 1941 is verified by my brothers, George and Bill, who recall going there for an afternoon YMCA Indian Guides gathering and hearing a startling announcement on a car radio (which was not a common accessory at that time) that the Japanese had just bombed a distant, relatively unheard-of place called Pearl Harbor in Hawaii, where it was early morning.

The next person these airmen met was a sheriff's deputy, who took charge of the rescue effort. In helping to explain why members of the crew seemed to be scattered all over the side of the mountain after they bailed out, John Wedesky declared that "the distance between you and the next man who bails out of an aircraft can be up to half a mile."

In spite of low battery problems and having to assemble all the crew members, they somehow made it down to the county sheriff's office, which at that time was located in the Santa Barbara County Courthouse. The rest of the crew arrived there at about noon. According to the *News-Press*,

"The eight [crewmen] suffered various degrees of cuts and bruises and were treated at Hoff [General Army] Hospital here." Neither of the surviving airmen recalled going there, however. Perhaps this was due to the trauma of a bailout into the darkness shrouding an unknown landscape just a few hours earlier. According to a letter from Robert M. Simpson, another member of the Thirty-fourth Bombardment Group but not one of the crew members on this plane, one of the men who bailed out broke a leg.

Hoff Hospital, as we used to call it, was located where part of the eighteen-hole Santa Barbara Golf Club is now. The only surviving road from that period is McCaw Avenue, which leads to the clubhouse and Mulligan's Restaurant from the intersection at Las Positas Road.

McCaw Avenue also approximates the path of the runway for one of Santa Barbara's earliest airports, the Casa Loma Field, which was established by pioneer aviator, aeronautical engineer, inventor and Thomas Edison laboratory assistant Earle L. Ovington (1879–1936), credited with being the first airmail pilot in the United States when he delivered, or rather dropped, a sack of it from an American-built Bleriot XI in 1911, on a "route" between Garden City and Mineola in New York, a distance of three miles. He later built a home, still in existence, in the nearby Samarkand Hills neighborhood but died before it was finished.

The Search for the Missing Crew Members of the *Hat in the Ring*

A fter lunch, the army transported the members of the crew to the site of the wreck, where they recovered various personal items and removed classified equipment from the wreckage. Later that evening, they were picked up by a B-17 Flying Fortress and flown to Bakersfield and then back to their base at Salinas.

But the drama of this incident had not quite ended. Early that morning, at 7:17 a.m. to be exact, three Liberators, also from the Thirty-fourth Bombardment Group based at Salinas but taking off from Bakersfield, began a search for the missing navigator and bombardier.

The planned route was to fly from Bakersfield to Santa Barbara and then to Point Conception. From this point, the search would continue heading in the direction of 34 degrees north, followed by 120 degrees and 30 minutes west, and then return to Santa Barbara. From here, the aircraft was to proceed to the Muroc Bombing Range (now Edwards Air Force Base), to Salinas, to Point Sur and then on to an air-to-air gunnery range at 36 degrees and 16 minutes north, followed by 122 degrees and 18 minutes west. Finally, after spending some time over the ocean, it would land at the Salinas Army Air Base at 4:19 p.m.

This occasion was not, however, a good time to look for people lost at sea because the typical July overcast near the coast and over the ocean ranged between altitudes of 300 and 1,600 feet.

At about 8:00 a.m., flight officer Vernon Stevens, the pilot of B-24E, 42-7160, radioed the Santa Barbara Airport control tower to advise that he was beginning the search pattern, but of course, he could see nothing between these altitudes. Descending through the marine layer, he hoped to emerge beneath the overcast and therefore have a better chance of spotting the missing airmen in the water.

According to the Report of Missing Aircraft, this plane was "last observed entering a low overcast over water south of Santa Cruz Island. Pilot entered this overcast in violation of definite instructions concerning weather flying."

In other words, the searching aircraft were forbidden to fly in areas of little or no visibility, at the risk of the mission suddenly ending in a "cumulo granite cloud." This phrase was used in a letter to me, almost half a century later, from the briefing officer of that mission, Robert M. Simpson.

Searching for the Searching Aircraft

Later that afternoon, this Liberator, with twelve men aboard, including an instructor pilot and a second navigator, was declared missing. There had been no communication from the aircraft since the contact with the Santa Barbara Airport tower that morning.

The next day, a massive search lasting several days was begun to find this missing B-24. The total endeavor included, at one time or another, a Coast Guard ship, eight navy ships, eleven B-24s, a PBY and a blimp, but low visibility weather conditions continued to hamper the effort.

Finally, on July 9, the search, having been expanded to a larger area, was called off; it was logically assumed that the plane had crashed somewhere in the vast expanse of the Pacific Ocean. Eight months would pass before a chance discovery revealed the fate of this bomber and its crew.

In the meantime, the war, even though it was slowly beginning to turn in our favor, was still raging in both Europe and the Pacific, and the training regimen, as well as the ships and aircraft, had to be focused in that direction.

The Board of Inquiry

A few days later, a board of inquiry, convened at the Salinas Army Air Base, determined that the cause of the accident involving the *Hat in the Ring* was due to 100 percent pilot error:

> *The pilot exercised poor judgment in not altering flight plan sufficiently to effect a landing before plane ran out of gas and also for not exercising proper cruise control (when excessive fuel consumption was first noted). It is believed that the pilot used good judgment in abandoning the plane (since the fuel was low and plane was over mountainous territory at night).*

In the report prepared after the accident, the copilot's statement, very similar to the pilot's, indicated that the first sign of trouble occurred some time after the mission began.

While the engineer provided a more detailed account about the fuel situation, as would be expected of an engineer, the mystery of the disappearing (and reappearing) fuel continued without explanation. He wrote:

> *When I shut the fuel valve "off" on No. 1 Engine, it had 375 gallons of gas in the tank. When the fuel ran considerably low in the other three tanks, I switched the No. 1 valve to the other tanks, and at that time I noticed there was [sic] only 100 gallons on the whole plane (according to the gauges). Just before we hit the Coast, there was [sic] 1200 gallons on board, and after circling Santa Barbara I looked again and found that 100 gallons was all that remained. There was [sic] no leaks on the inner wing or in the*

fuel lines because the Assistant and I checked that after noticing the large consumption of fuel.

In another report, the regional safety officer wrote, "1. Investigation disclosed cause of this accident to be abandonning [*sic*] ship by parachute due to running out of gasoline. This ship ran out of gasoline due to excessive fuel consumption through improper power settings. 2. Underlying cause was supervisory personnel's failure to properly instruct pilot in cruise power settings for aircraft."

In addition, the board had "no recommendation for action to prevent repetition" of this accident. Perhaps there are several reasons for this

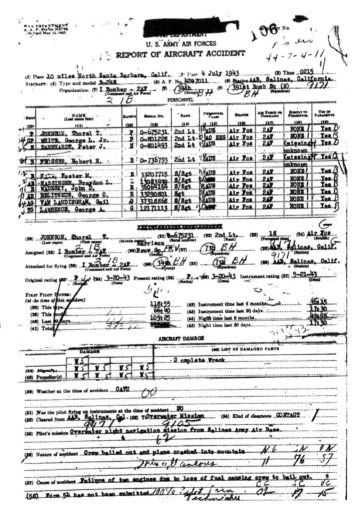

Page one of the Report of Aircraft Accident for B-24E, 42-7011, the *Hat in the Ring*, which crashed near Santa Barbara, California, on July 4, 1943. This is the censored version. An appeal to the secretary of the air force and a waiting period of two years were necessary to obtain the complete report. Document scanned by Bob Burtness.

conclusion. For example, there was a war on, and it was important to train crews as quickly as possible and send them into combat. And, of course, inexperienced crews were more likely to have accidents.

Further, the pilot of this aircraft had just under 119 hours flying Liberators, and most of those had been accumulated only during the previous three months. His total instrument time during the previous six months added up to 36¼ hours, and his nighttime flying hours totaled just under 44 hours during the same time period. It also appears that all of the crew members were in their twenties. The pilot was twenty-five years old, and at least three of the others were younger. Adding less than ideal weather conditions to this combination often resulted in a very challenging training environment and potentially disastrous outcomes for these crews.

While the board acknowledged that there was excessive fuel consumption, was it really due to incorrect power settings, or was it related to where the fuel was or was not? As former B-24 pilot Eugene Hartley once told me, transferring fuel from one tank to another was a tricky operation on these bombers. The cantankerous valves, almost at will, could be the cause of fuel leaks inside the airplane, decreased engine RPM, backfiring and, as cited previously, the erratic readings of the fuel gauges.

Another explanation, suggesting oil starvation, is implied in the *Santa Barbara News-Press* article of July 5, 1943, which reported that three "motors overheated and froze up." This assertion, however, has never been substantiated.

A third possibility is sabotage. In the opinion of officials of the Salinas Air Force Base, after the crew returned to Salinas, the entire Thirty-fourth Bombardment Group was grounded and never flew any further missions from that base. On the night the *Hat in the Ring* crashed, three other aircraft also went down, including one in Monterey Bay. As Gail stated in a letter to me, "We always thought that our airplane had something dumped into our fuel tanks."

The War Continues
Onward to China

On July 15, the crew departed Salinas by troop train and traveled to Biggs Army Airfield near El Paso, Texas, where the men arrived four days later. Here, the reconstituted crew, now with a replacement navigator (Lieutenant Harvey "Bill" Orr) and a new bombardier (Lieutenant John Bush), completed a third phase of training and also picked up a new aircraft, a B-24D, which they christened *Bob 'n Pete* (serial no. 42-40837?) in honor of their lost fellow crewmen, bombardier Robert Prosser and navigator Peter Dannhardt.

While the crew was at Biggs Field, at least one of them (but probably all of them) received a transient aircraft crew pass, dated July 26, 1943, which read:

> *The Bearer, _____ Rank, _____, ASN, _____ whose signature appears below, is a member of an aircraft crew of transient aircraft. He is authorized to leave and enter Biggs Field, Texas, only after properly identifying himself. This authorizes the bearer, if military or naval personnel, to visit Juarez, Mexico, in uniform, except between the hours of 11:00 P.M. and 10:00 A.M. This pass may be revoked at the discretion of the Base Commander.*

Departing El Paso on August 4, they flew to Lincoln, Nebraska, for final staging and had a seven-day furlough at this point.

Their scheduled departure on August 16 was delayed until 12:30 p.m. due to a wingtip clipping the tail of another airplane while taxiing out to the runway. This incident was caused by an air marshal who, for some unexplainable reason, directed the aircraft to pass too close to another one.

After the loss of the navigator and bombardier over the Santa Barbara Channel, the crew was reconstituted with replacements. Shown here is the "new crew" at Biggs Field in Texas prior to deploying to China. Behind the men is their new bomber, *Bob 'n Pete*, named in honor of their late comrades, Robert Prosser and Peter Dannhardt. In the background are two other bombers, a B-25 Mitchell and a B-17 Flying Fortress. This is probably a USAAF photograph. Photographer unknown.

While they were scheduled to fly to Prescott Island, Maine, they were diverted to Montreal, Canada, due to thunderstorm activity. They remained here until August 19 so that all systems on the aircraft could be completely checked out. The crew then flew on to Gander Lake, Newfoundland. Late in the evening on the following day, they began a long flight over the Atlantic Ocean and arrived in Ireland, near Belfast, the next morning. They remained there for a few days.

Continuing to Land's End, England, they then proceeded to Warrington, the site of an aircraft repair depot. They remained there for about two weeks until the landing gear was fixed. While this may seem like a long time for such a repair, there were apparently another fifteen or so aircraft there in the same situation. Also, the local mechanics were apparently not known for their speed in making such repairs. At any rate, the delay afforded the crew an opportunity to visit various places in England.

A Chain of Tragedies across Air, Land and Sea

This occasion included a two-week stay in Manchester, where the management of a local establishment called the Gomont Longbar arranged a standing table reservation for the crew.

After the repairs were completed, the crew then returned to Land's End and departed for Marrakech, Morocco, in North Africa. From here, they continued on to Algiers, Algeria, and Tripoli, Libya. The "airfield" in Tripoli was essentially a flat and very dusty place in the desert. After one aircraft landed, the next one had to wait for half an hour before it could do so. The one amenity that the crew did enjoy here, however, was a refreshing swimming pool at a British military installation.

The next stop was Cairo, Egypt, where they remained overnight so that a one-hundred-hour inspection could be performed on the aircraft's engines. While no problems were detected, crew member Vanlandingham remembered experiencing a painful toothache here. At the same location, John Wedesky remembered meeting a mess sergeant who asked the crew members to pick out any steak they saw on the table and he would prepare it to their liking. They were so impressed with his kindness that they thought they were in heaven. Apparently, some of them were so hungry that when he offered to do the same thing with another steak, they took him up on it.

The next destination was Abadan, Persia (now Iran), where the crew remained overnight. This city, by the way, is where Russian pilots came to pick up the U.S.-built Bell P-39 Airacobra fighter aircraft for combat operations against Germany.

The next day, the *Bob 'n Pete* crew flew to Karachi, India, and then on to Agra and Chabua, India. In Agra, Gail wound up in the hospital for two weeks with a case of trench mouth, and the new navigator had an epileptic fit, a condition that led to his being relieved from duty.

Since the crew could not continue to fly into China, especially over the very high Himalayan Mountains called "the Hump," it was necessary to wait for two weeks until the replacement navigator arrived. In the meantime, the rest of the crew took advantage of the delay by visiting two major attractions in Agra, the Taj Mahal and the Old Fort (also called the "Red Fort").

Flying over the Hump became necessary when the Japanese cut off the Burma Road, the only land route between India and China, in early 1942. This formidable series of mountain ranges and peaks, some of them three miles high, were challenging for even the most experienced pilots. While the air route between India and China was only 250 miles, the planes, with their heavy loads, had to be well above the highest elevations encountered because constant icing conditions and strong winds, especially down-draft situations, could easily drop an aircraft two thousand feet right into a jagged peak or side of a mountain, never to be found.

Such powerful forces of nature, especially the headwinds, could also make a 250-mile trip a very long one, and flying at higher and "safer" altitudes was potentially dangerous due to blizzard conditions, which could easily lead to straying off course, getting lost, running out of fuel or crashing into one of a multitude of mountainous obstacles. Adding to the complicated nature of such flights, there were no emergency landing fields along the way.

By the end of the war, more than 450 aircraft had been lost, and nearly eight hundred men had died along this treacherous "aluminum trail." This was the price for moving 740,000 tons of equipment, supplies (including gasoline) and other materiel (supplies and equipment) over the Hump on 167,285 trips. Wrecks continue to be periodically discovered to this day.

Arrival at Their New Home
and a Second Bailout

Finally, on October 14, 1943, the crew arrived at their new base in Yangkai, China, home of the 373rd Bombardment Squadron (Heavy). Yangkai was about forty-eight miles northeast of the newly formed 308th Bombardment Group (H) headquarters company in Kunming, which was also the headquarters of the 14th Air Force.

This bombardment group, however, had been in the China-Burma-India area of operations since September 1942 and would remain until November 1945. Its motto, "Percussus Resurgo," means, "When Struck Down I Rise Again." This was in reference to the organization's ability to continue growing in spite of its losses. On its emblem was an image of Medusa, one of three Gorgon sisters capable, among other things, of overcoming any opposition.

Yangkai, one of the bases in this organization, was situated at an elevation of about 6,200 feet and was therefore probably in a cooler, more comfortable climate than installations at lower elevations. Twelve B-24 crews were stationed there, and they were attached to the Chinese army, which provided mess arrangements and houseboys to maintain their rooms.

There were logistical problems here, though. The China bases were dependent on supplies and materials, including bombs and ammunition, flown in from airfields in India, but construction of these installations was slow due to excessive rainfall, a short supply of native laborers (who had fled the area in the wake of Japanese air attacks) and the lack of construction equipment arriving in a timely manner. This situation therefore obligated the 308th Bombardment Group to bring in its own supplies from the growing stockpile in India.

In fairness to the native laborers, however, one should consider the following comments, prophetic in part, expressed by Major Max. R. Fennell, a veteran airline pilot and commanding officer of the 513th Bombardment Squadron (B-17), who noted in the 1944 work *Born in Battle: Round the World Adventures of the 513th Bombardment Squadron* the industry of how large numbers of coolies rapidly repaired runway damage after Japanese bombardments:

> *The Chinese give homemade bombs to their own pilots to take out and drop on the Japs. When the Japs return the compliment, about ten thousand coolies are waiting to repair the damage. Each coolie carries a little sack of stones. After the bombings they run out on the runway and fill up the bomb craters with the stones from their sacks.*
>
> *I have seen ten thousand coolies by sheer manpower repair the most devastating destruction in fifteen minutes. After the war is over and these traits in the Chinese character are put to work for constructive organization, China will rise as one of the World's greatest nations.*

If the materiel were destined for other Fourteenth Air Force bases in China, such as the installations in Kiangsi and Fukian Provinces, it had to be transported by other modes, too; these included trucks, a narrow-gauge railroad, junks and sampans. In short, it was a primitive supply line, but it worked. There were no other choices.

Living conditions in Yangkai were not the best, though. Since the supplies brought in from India were primarily intended for the war effort, local resources were exploited to help meet their needs. This situation helped to make ox meat and potatoes a primary part of their diet. Eggs were available, too, and the cook did an excellent job under these circumstances.

On the other hand, the PX (the Post Exchange) was open for only half a day each month. Personnel were allotted only so many candy bars and packs of cigarettes and "that was it." No beer or soda pop was available, and whiskey wasn't either, except for some bootlegged liquor called "Uma Wine." Claimed to be the creation of "European experts," it was actually made in China. One cannot help but ask if this was a sign of things that would be happening on the world economic stage in the next century.

Their living conditions were further described by Braydon Hassinger in a letter to neighboring friends that was printed in his hometown newspaper on January 20, 1944:

Tail gunner George Lawrence and armor gunner (top and waist positions) Gail Vanlandingham. This photo was probably taken at the crew's Yangkai, China base. Photographer unknown.

First engineer Foster Hare. This photograph was probably taken at the crew's Yangkai, China base. Photographer unknown.

Bombardier John Bush, navigator Howard Kirkland and pilot Thorel Johnson. This photo was probably taken at their base in Yangkai, China. Photographer unknown.

I am in China now, getting a kick in at the Japs now and then. I am in a heavy bomber outfit and like the work very much.

China, this place in China anyway, is very nice. The weather is what I like. It is the cold season now. The only thing is that it just doesn't get very cold. I don't think it has been below zero yet. Usually every morning when we get up the ground is covered with frost. There is never much snow. It has snowed only once since I have been here.

The only trouble with being away from the United States is that we miss so many things. Of course, we miss our friends, but its [sic] the little things that make us realize that we are not in the States. When I say little things, I mean those that we never think about such as a cake, candy bar, or milk shake.

Another method of communicating with the homefront was by V-Mail, which, in the words of former POW William R. Livingstone, was

a letter form provided by the Army and used by millions of overseas GIs during WWII. The Army photographed them and flew the undeveloped film back to the states. There, they developed it, printed each letter on to a 4¼ by 5" piece of photo paper, and mailed them. This is what the folks at home received—tiny writing, and only one page.

A Chain of Tragedies across Air, Land and Sea

While probably everyone on the crew took advantage of this medium, there is a record of at least one example, dated November 15, 1943, sent by radio operator/gunner George Belitskus to his brother, Frank, and his wife, who lived in Cuddy, Pennsylvania, at that time. Complete with old English lettering and graphics showing holly, a soldier and the three Wise

DEAR BOB:
   MY COUSIN RECENTLY DISCOVERED AN ORIGINAL V-MAIL IN ONE
OF HER LATE FATHER'S BOOKS APPARENTLY FROM CHINA
DATED NOV. 15, 1943, FROM MY FATHER S/SGT. GEORGE C.
BELITSKUS, TO HIS BROTHER FRANK BELITSKUS AND HIS
WIFE WIFE WHO LIVED IN CUDDY, PA. U.S.A., FOR THE
CHRISTMAS HOLIDAY SEASON OF 1943.
   I THOUGHT YOU MIGHT BE INTERESTED IN THIS SMALL
BIT OF HISTORY, GEORGE SR. WAS A RADIO OPERATOR
AND GUNNER ON A B-24 BOMBER IN CHINA.
   KEEP IN TOUCH . . . .
                              GEORGE C. BELITSKUS
              PHONE # 412-221-5104

This copy of a V-Mail ("Victory") letter was a Christmas greeting sent by George Belitskus to his brother, Frank, in 1943. The note below it was written by George's son and sent to me in 2007. The document was scanned by Bob Burtness.

57

Men riding their camels, the message reads, "The Season's Greetings, The United States Army Forces in China Burma India, May the Christ child make your Christmas happy and may this happiness overflow into the New Year." That this V-Mail was dated almost six weeks before Christmas suggests that Sergeant Belitskus wanted to ensure that his brother and sister-in-law received this greeting in a timely manner.

While thoughts about home, family and friends were great morale boosters, the airmen were nevertheless obligated to face the realities and their attendant uncertainties of warfare, including both the long periods of boredom and the brief moments of sheer terror.

At about the first of the following year, 1944, about five of the aircraft from this base were sent on a mission over French Indochina (now known, chiefly, as Vietnam). Later that night, and without explanation, the remaining crews were suddenly awakened and told to prepare to leave. They then embarked on an all-night trip by truck to a place by a lake up in the mountains northwest of Kunming. Arriving there the next morning, they were then told that they would be there for a one-week rest because none of the five aircraft here mentioned had returned from the mission. Once again, the calamities of war earned the remaining airmen a well-deserved rest. Some of them also acquired sunburns in the process.

Upon returning to Yangkai, they flew a number of missions from forward bases, such as Kwailin, where they were attacked by Japanese Betty bombers, and Chentu, from where they embarked on missions to skip bomb and strafe Japanese shipping, as well as land targets.

Target strafing, normally executed by fighters, was an unusual bomber tactic developed by Major General Claire Chennault, whose legendary American Volunteer Group (AVG), better known as the Flying Tigers, harassed Japanese operations in China both before and after the Pearl Harbor attack in late 1941. The group eventually became the Fourteenth Air Force, which was the smallest of the numbered air forces but had the largest area of responsibility. Other target destinations included Shanghai, Hong Kong, Canton, Hangkow and Hainan Island in China, Hanoi (in what was then called French Indochina) and even the Philippines.

On one of these missions, when the bomber attacked an airfield, John Wedesky saw a lone Japanese truck driver attempting to escape from the falling bombs. "I was actually rooting for him to make it, but he didn't," stated Wedesky, who was manning a machine gun at the time. Like so many others involved "up close and personal" in the war, he nevertheless had a job to do and did it to help rescue a nation threatened by hostile powers.

A Chain of Tragedies across Air, Land and Sea

After a number of these combat missions, however, the *Bob 'n Pete* crew had to give up its cherished Liberator because the self-sealing fuel tanks had been punctured so many times by enemy fire that the leaks could not be repaired. This meant that while the aircraft could not be flown again, parts of it could be "cannibalized" and used to keep other B-24s in the air. One of their subsequent aircraft was named *Nip Nipper.*

It must be stated here that the risks of war were not limited to the missions to, over and from the targets—home bases were always subject to retaliation. For example, following a number of attacks on Japanese installations, an enemy force of thirty bombers and forty fighters descended on the Fourteenth Air Force headquarters at Kunming and could have completely destroyed it were it not for the poor accuracy of their bombardiers. There were efforts to attack these bases by land also.

In the meantime, the crew was about to experience another major event in their military aviation careers. On the night of February 5, 1944, they were assigned to fly to Bangkok, Thailand, with four other aircraft on a ten-hour mission. An alternate target area may have been Rangoon, Burma, which was about the same distance from their base.

According to a newspaper article, published by the Army Air Forces Training Command just over a year later on Friday, April 6, 1945, the crew boarded its assigned aircraft, a B-24 called *For Sale*, and embarked on what was to be their thirteenth mission—this did, in fact, turn out to be an unlucky one. The name of their aircraft, however, has also been identified as *Flamingo II*, B-24J, 42-72835, according to an online obituary for Robert Prosser. This dilemma raises the unlikely possibility that the plane had two names.

This flight, possibly called Mission 57, was without another of the original crew members, assistant radio operator George C. Belitskus. His son, George C. Belitskus Jr., wrote that his father was sent on a mission over the South China Sea "sometime during 1944" when their aircraft was shot down by the Japanese.

While the crew was picked up by one of our submarines, George suffered a broken back when he landed hard in the water because his parachute did not fully open. This injury resulted in his being sent home, and it was necessary for him to wear a steel back brace for the rest of his life, during which time he was on 100 percent disability. A copy of a postcard photograph, furnished by his son, shows George (in uniform and using a walking stick) and his brother, John, in front of what could be a large hospital building in Hot Springs, Arkansas, on September 14, 1944.

Since no other members, or their children, of the original crew mentioned this incident, perhaps he was a substitute for the radio operator of another Liberator crew that had the unlucky day. Hence, George Belitskus's mission, while probably not his thirteenth one, turned out to be an unlucky one nonetheless.

The rest of the crew, now aboard *For Sale/Flamingo II*, encountered bad weather shortly after departing the base, a situation that would plague them for the rest of the mission. Under these conditions, the theory, according to the manual, was to fly forty-five degrees off-course for one minute and then fly forty-five degrees in the opposite direction for another minute. Everyone would presumably be back together at this point.

As John Wedesky remembered, though:

> *That's when the trouble really started…The weather was so bad the entire formation had to split up. Each plane headed for the target separately. It was a long, lonely haul, but our navigator got us there right on the button. Since the weather was still bad, we had to come in low to identify the target. By the time we had our bombs away their flak had got to us, and we found ourselves in a hell of a fix.*

On this mission, Gail Vanlandingham recalled that since each plane reached the target at different times, "one, or both, of the other planes… ahead of us…They were ready for us with search lights and anti-aircraft. We dropped our bombs and got out of there. We had taken several hits but no one was hurt."

Even though no one was injured during this raid (flown at an altitude of five thousand feet, according to the Individual Casualty Questionnaires prepared later), "the value of the ship," according to Technical Sergeant James Walker's newspaper article written a year later, "had been reduced to that of a leaky rowboat, minus oars, caught in a riptide." It was time to turn for home.

THE SECOND BAILOUT: OVER ENEMY TERRITORY

Along the way, though, the navigator determined that they were lost. In the meantime, a navigator contacted in another bomber advised them to "home in" on him, but he was obliged to admit, half an hour later, that he was lost, too.

According to the later recollections of George L. White III, copilot George White's son, "Weather again played a factor. The navigator couldn't get a good [celestial] fix. They could [not] descend too low because of the mountainous terrain."

Finally, after overflying their base by two to three hundred miles and being off-course by about one thousand miles to the east, due to an unknown strong wind from the west, they continued flying until the aircraft ran out of fuel. Once again, radio operator Wedesky was unable to establish contact with anyone, and once again they found it necessary to leave the aircraft.

While the time was about two o'clock in the morning, the same as it had been when they bailed out near Santa Barbara, they were not over the friendly territory of Santa Barbara County. Instead, it was in the mountains northwest of Chengdu, not far from the Wuylang River, an area of China occupied by the Japanese.

As John Wedesky later declared, "We crammed our pockets full of K rations, made a last-minute equipment check and then, one by one, we jumped."

The Long Journey to Freedom

While everyone safely parachuted from the doomed bomber at an altitude of about eighteen thousand feet above a mountainous area northwest of Chengdu, China, it was not under the most ideal of conditions. As before, their descent was happening during the very early morning, but here they landed on snow-covered slopes at an elevation of about nine thousand feet. They were also in enemy territory.

Each crew member was equipped with "blood chits," also called identification or rescue flags, sewn on their flight jackets (first on the outside, then later on the inside since the Communists and the Nationalists were enemies). In addition to an illustration of the Nationalist Chinese flag was the statement, written in Chinese, "This foreign person has come to China to help in the war effort. Soldiers and civilians, one and all, should rescue, protect, and provide him with medical care."

Rescuers were generally given some kind of a reward, which varied from trinkets and food to silver, gold or money, the value of which would be determined by the amount of rescue effort involved. Payment was to be made by either a local government entity or the Nationalist government.

As John Wedesky approached the earth beneath his oscillating parachute, the hard, snow-covered surface of a mountaintop "suddenly rushed up to him." Upon landing, he found himself at the top of a snowcapped mountain still in the clouds. He arrived alive, once again, but he was both alone and lost. When there was enough light to see, several hours later, he buried his parachute to help avoid detection by any enemy forces in the area. He then cautiously "walked" down the mountain by the seat of his pants and hoped

A Chain of Tragedies across Air, Land and Sea

This "blood chit," used by crew member Braydon Hassinger, was also known as an identification or rescue flag. Sewn on to their flight jackets, it showed the Nationalist Chinese flag plus a statement, written in Chinese: "This foreign person has come to China to help in the war effort. Soldiers and civilians, one and all, should rescue, protect, and provide him with medical care." A reward of some type was to be made by either the local or Nationalist government. *Photo by Jana Churchwell.*

Technical Sergeant John Wedesky was the radio operator with the original Johnson crew that parachuted from the *Hat in the Ring* over Santa Barbara. This apparently official U.S. Army Air Forces photo was emailed to me by Marc McDonald.

to meet the other members of the crew before continuing on what was to be a long journey. At the bottom, he found himself on a trail. Equipped with a "Pointie-Talkie" army language book in one hand and his .45-caliber automatic pistol in the other, he cautiously proceeded along this path.

Later approaching a small village that, fortunately, was inhabited by Chinese, he was met by an enthusiastic group of residents that escorted him to a most welcome warming fire, as well as the navigator resting beside it. As John recalled, "It was sure good to see him. All we did for the next three days was eat fats and rice and sweat out the rest of the crew. During that time, four of them were found and brought in."

Apparently, during John's first meal since the bailout, he was offered some chicken soup that included the head of the chicken. Considered a delicacy and the best part of the soup, he was obliged to accept it because refusal would have been interpreted as an insult. After all, his hosts were doing their best to accommodate their guests. As John later reflected, "You had to do what you had to do."

About a week later, at another village, the group joined up with the other four members of the crew. "We were pretty lucky," John later exclaimed. "And no one was seriously hurt. However getting back to our base was quite a job. The Chinese were wonderful, and we'll never forget the debt we owe them for all the help they gave us. But even so, the next twenty-three days of walking and riding on burros over the mountains and through the wilds of inland China was not a pleasant experience."

Among the members of the second group of four crewmen was Gail Vanlandingham. Upon landing, he rolled up in his parachute and waited for daylight. When it arrived, he climbed about forty feet to the top of a ridge, hollered and saw another crew member, Foster Hare, in a tree across the canyon. They agreed to meet farther down the canyon in the shelter of a group of trees. Due to the rugged terrain, however, it took about two hours to get there. Once there, they encountered two more crew members, Braydon Hassinger and George White.

From this point, they climbed a nearby ridge, from which Gail saw a hut below. Once again, it was "make a decision" time. While the men needed help in a number of different ways, they did not know, at this point, whether they were in friendly territory or not. Gail asked them to cover him with the only weapons they had, their pistols.

When he arrived at the hut, he encountered an old man, an old woman and a boy of about seventeen. They did not speak English, and the other two crew members, who were now at the hut, did not speak Chinese. They were also not friendly toward the Americans, and they did not, for example, even allow Gail into their home to dry his shoes after he fell down a waterfall. At this point, the men feared that these people, due to their unfriendly attitudes, would turn them in to the Japanese. One crewman suggested killing them, a tactic taught in their survival training, but the others resisted the idea.

Here, the "Pointie-Talkie" booklets, issued with other survival gear, contained basic questions in English and Chinese on the left-hand pages and the answers on the right-hand pages. But if the people to whom they were shown did not speak or read Chinese, as was the case here, these booklets were useless. Thus, not knowing where they were, not knowing where the Japanese were and being limited to sign language communication raised the cause for concern, especially with natives exhibiting a questionable friendliness.

Finally, the boy took Gail into the hut so that he could dry his shoes by the fire. After a little while, he emerged from the hut and announced to the others, "Guys, they're friendly!" Consequently, this crisis ended, and everyone was relieved.

As it turned out, the Chinese, understandably, were afraid of the strangely dressed newcomers who spoke peculiar foreign sounds. But after they became better acquainted through some nonverbal communication, the tense situation dramatically improved. Using sign language, the boy explained that there was a city down the mountain. He then escorted the crew members two to three miles down a trail to a village of about five hundred people and later returned to his home.

Again using sign language, the men learned that another village was situated farther down the trail, and they decided to continue their trek. The trail, about four feet wide, was located in a scenic canyon that was only about a hundred feet wide but one thousand feet deep.

During a rest stop, they encountered a dignified-looking old man dressed in a long robe and cotton shoes. He was also wearing a felt hat of a type that one might see in the United States. He, too, communicated with the crew members in sign language and pretended that he understood the language used in their book; in actuality, however, he did not. But the Chinese flags sewn on their flight jackets and the fact that they were AVG's (American Volunteer Group) must have successfully communicated to the old man that they were friendly. He may have also known that the USAAF offered monetary rewards, sometimes up to $15,000, to those who rescued American aviators.

As a result, he invited them to come to his village to enjoy his hospitality, which included a delicious meal of rice, meat and chicken. This was a pleasant change from the only thing they had to eat after bailing out, a little hard chocolate. Their hosts, in turn, relished the last of the crewmen's cigarettes.

The next morning, the men continued walking down the mountain via a series of stair steps built into the trail until they reached the next village, where they slept on straw. It was also the custom here for the natives to literally live with their animals.

Along the way, Gail developed the habit of asking every new person he met if he or she could speak English. The constant response was a confused expression until he encountered a boy who entered a hut on the following afternoon where the crew had stopped to warm themselves. When the boy announced that he did speak English, Gail was so happy that he hugged him.

The crew learned that they were in Japanese territory and that the enemy patrolled the area about once a week; they had been there just two days before. Farther down the trail was a city where Chinese volunteer soldiers (guerrillas) could help them. Arriving there that night at about nine o'clock, the men were housed in a building with beds made of boards about six inches off the floor. There were also charcoal grills around them to help take the chill out of the winter air. Exhausted from the day's journey, the crew had no trouble falling asleep.

When he awoke the following morning, however, Gail was surprised to discover, standing over him, a white man dressed in a robe, a square hat and a collar that appeared to be worn backward. Sensing that he was looking at an apparition, he feared that he had died during the night. But when he asked the man who he was, the response was, "I am Father Hawk. Where are you from?" The airmen concluded that they were at a mission, and Father Hawk turned out to be a German Catholic priest working there with three other priests, all of whom hosted the men for nine days and fed them well. At night, however, they were obligated to stay at the local Chinese garrison, in facilities that were "next to nothing." The beds, for example, were wooden platforms covered with cotton quilts.

After the remaining members of the crew arrived, Father Hawk quipped that they had caused the price of eggs to triple twice because they were eating so many of them. On the night before they were to leave and continue down the mountain, the crew was introduced to five or six nuns, who had been preparing the meals during the entire length of their stay and also repaired and cleaned the airmen's clothing. Gail did not wear Chinese clothing just during this time—for a much longer period, he also wore Chinese shoes since his flying boots were irreparably damaged by a warming fire that apparently "warmed" them a little too much.

A Chain of Tragedies across Air, Land and Sea

The entire crew was very grateful for the help provided by the missionaries and the sisters and concluded that the latter group had been hidden from view most of the time for "their protection."

En route, they met a man named Fong Sen Ching, who became their guide during the rest of the trip. For some unknown reason, however, he quickly developed a reputation for not telling the truth. Whenever he told them that he would be truthful in the future, he soon told another lie. This unnerving experience created some fears among the crewmen because, after all, they were still in enemy territory. Unfortunately, guides were in short supply.

While walking was probably the primary mode of their transportation, animals such as burros were also periodically used during their journey, according to John Wedesky. At some point during this period, four horses were made available to crewmen who had riding experience. While Gail was one of these individuals, he happened to draw the least trained animal. After mounting the animal, he tapped it on the side of the head to turn, but its immediate crow hopping/bucking response continued even after he hastily dismounted, and it did not stop until the horse had raced up a nearby hill. Gail decided to walk on his own to the next village. When he arrived, the others had been waiting for him for two hours at a private home where they were to spend the night.

Here the crew awoke earlier than anticipated the next morning to a lot of smoke in the air. The warming fire in the room's charcoal grill had burned through the floor and set the house on fire—thus ending the "central heating system" and what had begun as a restful and peaceful night.

Finally, when the men had the chance to ride in vehicles during their long trek, it was in trucks powered by charcoal. Traveling at night, these vehicles could not go in reverse. Therefore, whenever a sharp curve in the road was encountered, it would be necessary for everyone to get out and push them back and forth a few times to get around the curve.

Each vehicle had a "pilot" and "copilot." The pilot drove, and the copilot took care of the other things to help keep things moving. For example, he had to put gas into the carburetor in order to go up a hill. Since there were no brakes, wooden pyramids with handles were placed behind the rear wheels.

Once they were able to cross the Wuyang River, they would no longer be in Japanese-held territory because this location was the southern boundary of the territory captured by the Japanese. In this city, they met some government officials and girls who treated and fed them well and helped them plan their escape. Just before midnight, they concealed themselves in the bed of a hay truck and prayed that no one would be skewered by the Japanese guards' probing bayonets.

After a successful river crossing, they continued riding to a point where they were dropped off; they continued walking until reaching Fushun, a walled city that, due to security reasons, was closed to entry until about seven o'clock in the morning. Arriving there well before the gates opened, they nevertheless had to patiently wait until they were granted permission to enter the city, where they would feel more secure and comfortable.

In the meantime, they attempted to keep warm by setting a building on fire with mosquito repellent, but it would not work. Perhaps this effort was inspired by their previous experience in the home where the "central heating system" had "gone wild" early one morning and obliged them to hastily depart before it engulfed the entire structure in flames.

Finally, when the city gates opened, some local government officials helped them find accommodations at a local hotel, where they stayed for two days. They undoubtedly enjoyed some comforts here that they had not had in a long time.

Perhaps it was in Fushun where a surviving photograph was taken of the crew and their hosts before continuing on their journey. Seven of the original ten crew members are in this photo, including Thorel "Skip" Johnson, George White, George Lawrence, Foster Hare, Gail Vanlandingham, John Wedesky and Braydon Hassinger.

They then boarded a train and rode until it derailed, perhaps due to an open switch in a railroad yard. The car the airmen were riding in ended up on its side, but the only injury happened to John Wedesky when he was stuck on the head by a falling fan. Sixty-four stitches were required to close the wound.

The trip to Kweilin was made by truck, and from this point they flew to Kunming. From here, they rode in a truck back to their base at Yangkai, where officials were surprised to see them. None of the messages sent ahead by the crew, now listed as missing (a fact that had also been telegrammed to their parents), ever reached its destination. On February 29, after the crew had returned to its base, Sergeant Hassinger was able to send a cable to his mother to advise her that he was "safe and well." Presumably, the other crew members did the same.

There had been some tough times during this twenty-three-day ordeal, including periods of cold and hunger that resulted in weight loss in everyone. Gail's, in particular, dropped from a normal 175 pounds to 128, a loss of 47

The "walkout photo." After spending twenty-three days in the Japanese-held portion of China, the crew celebrated its escape, in part, with this photo. Seven of the original *Hat in the Ring* crew members are included: pilot Thorel Johnson (in the center of the back row), radio operator John Wedesky (on Johnson's right), copilot George White and tail gunner George Lawrence (on White's left). In the front row (from left to right) are first engineer Foster Hare, armor gunner Gail Vanlandingham and second engineer Braydon Hassinger (wearing his flight jacket). The replacement crew members are navigator Howard Kirkland (on Johnson's left), gunner Charles Dealy (below Johnson) and bombardier John Bush (on the far right in the front row). Photographer unknown.

pounds! In the wake of this lengthy and harrowing experience, the navigator, who had done a good job on the many missions flown, refused to return to duty because the ordeal "had taken too much out of him."

Once back at the base, the crew learned that of the five crews that took off on the night of their last mission, three of them went down and two were never heard from again. Again the men were lucky. They had now successfully bailed out of doomed bombers twice, one of those occasions being over enemy territory. Before their tour of duty was over, however, there was more work to do. Placed on detached service with the Tenth Air Force near Calcutta, India, they flew missions that included bombing Rangoon and laying mines in the Bangkok, Thailand harbor.

After the crew returned to China, radio operator John Wedesky was again injured as he departed on a mission with a different crew whose aircraft crashed on takeoff. This event forced the top turret to fall out of its position and hit the top of his head, scalping him from the front to the back. Lying on the back of his head, it was attached only by the skin at the rear. After flopping it back into place, he spent the next three weeks recuperating in a hospital. At this point, one gets the impression that John was jinxed. After returning to Yangkai, he participated on more combat missions, which, fortunately, were uneventful. Later, he and the other enlisted crew members returned to the United States, but the pilot and other officers remained at the base for a while longer.

Unraveling the San Miguel Island Mystery Eleven Years Later

Thus, while the crew of the *Hat in the Ring/Eddie Rickenbacker*, *Bob 'n Pete*, *For Sale/Flamingo II* and the *Nip Nipper* survived the war intact, in spite of some harrowing experiences and close calls, there were a few other events relating to their first bailout near Santa Barbara. One of these occurred about nine months after an intensive search was conducted to find the missing navigator and bombardier. The second one happened eleven years later. Both revolve around the search plane that disappeared fairly early on its mission.

Flashback to San Miguel Island. As the northernmost member of the Channel Islands off the coast of Santa Barbara long used for raising sheep, this island was taken over by the navy and used as a lookout station after the war began. On March 16, 1944, some station personnel who happened to be in the vicinity of Green Mountain, located only about a mile from their installation, discovered a military aircraft wreck that turned out to be the B-24E search plane that vanished the previous July.

Crashing on a shallow slope at the 500-foot level on the northeast side of the 831-foot-high mountain, the highest elevation on the island, the aircraft was undoubtedly in a low overcast, and the pilot could not see the sudden fate that awaited him and his crew.

On the day after this discovery, a navy vessel was dispatched from Santa Barbara so that the bodies of the twelve airmen could be recovered and turned over to the army for burial. At the same time, items of a military nature, such as "radios, ammunition, machine guns and turrets," were salvaged. A few days later, the case of this missing aircraft was closed, but the drama of the incident was not over, and it would not end until another ten years had passed.

Let us now fast-forward to September 1954, when a group of hikers, or two couples, spent a pleasant late summer day exploring the natural beauties of San Miguel Island and searching for Indian relics, according to one newspaper account. Returning to their boat, anchored in one of the coves, they found themselves walking through an area scattered with old military aircraft wreckage. Looking more closely, they discovered what appeared to be human bones and concluded that they were at the site of an unreported aircraft wreck.

After returning to the mainland, they reported the find to authorities, who passed the information on to the air force, which could not, at that point, locate any records of a missing aircraft on San Miguel Island. The reported policy at that time was to transfer such records into the retired files after five years. There was official interest in the case, however, because two Liberators missing from Fresno's Hammer Field (now called the Fresno Yosemite International Airport) during the war had never been accounted for. Perhaps this one would turn out to be one of those bombers. Plans were therefore made to launch an investigation with the hope of unraveling this mystery. At this time, a helicopter from Norton Air Force Base, near San Bernardino, flew to San Miguel Island to identify the wreckage.

Later, on October 2, shortly after midnight, a twelve-person identification team consisting of nine men (including civilians Robert W. Ralston and George J. Schwaderer plus seven enlisted men) from the Air Force Memorial Affairs Branch, Identification Section of the Air Materiel Command at Wright-Patterson Air Force Base in Dayton, Ohio, as well as three medical personnel from Norton Air Force Base, San Bernardino, California, left Los Angeles Harbor aboard the 125-foot-long Coast Guard cutter the *Morris*, which headed for San Miguel Island in calm seas.

However, early the following morning, when it was about five miles offshore from Point Mugu, it inexplicably collided with a sixty-foot-long ketch, the *Aloha*, as it sailed from its homeport of Santa Barbara to Newport Beach. Penetrated nearly four feet in the midsection by the *Morris*, the *Aloha* quickly sank in about one minute, probably due to both the large hole thus created and its ten-ton lead keel. This accident cost the lives of two of the five people aboard the pleasure craft, including the skipper's wife, Bea Caspers, age twenty-six, and another crew member, Harold Kelley, age sixty-one. The skipper, Ronald Caspers, age twenty-seven, who was also the owner's son, was at the helm at the time of the collision. Described as an excellent sailor, he later explained the cause of the accident as a "nighttime illusion with the running lights. It did not look to me like the cutter was moving."

After rescuing the three others from the very chilly water, the crew of the *Morris* immediately returned to Los Angeles with the survivors and departed once again for San Miguel Island later that afternoon. In the meantime, both navy and Coast Guard aircraft spent eleven to twelve hours searching the area for the two missing individuals. Their remains were never found.

The next day, the cutter arrived at the island, and members of the air force team hiked to the fan-shaped one-acre site of the wreckage, which they immediately ascertained was a B-24 Liberator. The aircraft's tail number, still visible in spite of being exposed to the sun and the salt air for eleven years, enabled them to positively identify the wreck as the aircraft that searched for the two downed airmen in 1943. A memorandum prepared after this investigation noted, "Several photographs have been taken by Base Investigators. A few scattered bones were located; sand is covering most of the remains. The fuselage is broken into four parts."

The case was finally closed after the air force ultimately determined, following an intense records check, that the bomber wreck had been found once before. A *Los Angeles Times* article, dated March 20, 1944, cited the discovery of the wreck. This event was confirmed in another *Times* article, dated October 3, 1954, by two former sailors, Robert McKee and Stan Sokolis (both assigned to a radio unit on the island), who discovered the wreckage and helped with the salvage work eleven years earlier. There was other publicity, written in 1944, about this event, including an Arizona newspaper article cited in the bibliography here. It therefore appears that only the records were missing during the previous ten years.

At this point, one may wonder about the reason why the search plane chose to violate the rule that forbade flying in an area with low or no visibility. Among the twelve crew members were three pilots, the pilot and copilot plus a command/instructor pilot, whose role was to be in charge of the aircraft.

This individual, First Lieutenant Douglas Thornburg, who two years before joined the U.S. Army Air Corps, as it was then called, had the same responsibility on another Liberator that crashed during a training mission only three weeks earlier. Six men lost their lives on that mission, while four others, including Lieutenant Thornburg, successfully parachuted from the ailing aircraft just before it crashed. Before he bailed out, he told the copilot, who was flying the plane, that it was time to leave. In addition, there were two other crew members attempting to help a third man, whose parachute was caught in the waist door opening, all of this in a rapidly changing

Tail of B-24E, 42-27119, which crashed in Weed, California, on June 10, 1943, during a training mission. Six of the airmen lost their lives, but four others parachuted to safety. One of them was command/instructor and pilot First Lieutenant Douglas Thornburg, who died three weeks later on San Miguel Island when the search plane he commanded crashed on Green Mountain. *Photo by John and Lew Funk, courtesy of Jana Churchwell, niece of the copilot who perished on 42-27119.*

environment of losing altitude with no lights and no working intercom. In the end, these four plus two others did not make it.

The thought of losing these six airmen may have been on Lieutenant Thornburg's mind when the searching aircraft under his command entered the overcast near Santa Cruz Island. Perhaps he wanted the plane to be low enough in order to see and save two airmen who had bailed out of the *Hat in the Ring* just a few hours before. Presumably under pressure to do something, he was undoubtedly aware of the risks involved but nevertheless took the chance with the hope that these downed flyers would be spotted.

Unfortunately, the gamble cost twelve lives whose military service careers abruptly ended, but the war continued for everyone else, at least until newspaper headlines such as "World Peace, Japs' Defeat" appeared.

The fate of the two other missing Liberators mentioned previously had been learned by the end of the decade. One of them was discovered in 1955 at the bottom of Huntington Lake, which is about sixty miles east of Fresno. The other was located in 1960 in a small Sierra Nevada lake about twenty miles southwest of Bishop.

The Crew Members and What Became of the Survivors After the War

The Liberators that carried this crew, and replacement crew members, on their training and combat missions appear to add up to five different aircraft, but this count may not be accurate. From what is known and can be documented, the *Hat in the Ring*, as Gail Vanlandingham called it, was used for training until it crashed behind the coastal mountains in Santa Barbara County.

Another written description refers to this aircraft as the *Eddie Rickenbacker*. A surviving photograph shows the plane with all four engines running beside a hangar, possibly during a test run-up at Ford's Willow Run plant near Detroit, Michigan, where this aircraft was manufactured.

This photograph also shows the *Hat in the Ring* logo on the forward part of the fuselage, the usual place for nose art. This is unique, however, because such illustrations were usually added later when the aircraft was assigned to a combat unit.

The next plane, the *Bob 'n Pete*, was flown to China and used on a number of combat missions until the fuel tanks had so many bullet and flak holes that it could no longer be used. Parts of it were cannibalized to help keep other Liberators in the air.

Nip Nipper (B-24D, 42-40391) was also used on combat missions. Flown by another crew, it reportedly crashed in French Indochina in 1945. Another story, also unsubstantiated, claims that this aircraft crashed in Kurmitola, India. For the record, there is a photograph, showing another crew (unidentified) in front of this bomber, in the 1989 issue of the *Annual Pictorial Magazine of the Flying Tigers of the 14th Air Force Association*.

There are photographs of these three aircraft, and the latter two also show the crew posed in front of them. In addition, *Nip Nipper* is illustrated in *Chennault's Forgotten Warriors* by Carroll V. Glines. The number of bombs painted on its fuselage indicates that this bomber was a veteran of thirty combat missions when the photograph was taken.

For Sale, according to a newspaper article written about John Wedesky just over a year after the incident, was the name of the bomber from which the crew members bailed out over China after returning from a mission, their thirteenth, to Bangkok, Thailand. Another account identifies this aircraft as the *Flamingo II* (42-40038 or 42-72835). This explanation, however, has not been substantiated.

One possible explanation for all of the confusion about which plane did what and where could be due to the same aircraft having different names at different times. According to Jana Churchwell (who has been extensively researching the histories of B-24 Liberator crews, especially the one on which her uncle was the copilot), it did not happen often, but it did occur.

Overall, the B-24 Liberators, in spite of all of their deficiencies, accumulated an impressive record against the enemy. As 14th Air Force Commander General Claire Chennault declared in his praise of both the 308th Bombardment Group and the Liberators in his book, *Way of a Fighter*:

> *The 308th was unique among heavy bomb groups. It was entirely self-supporting across the Hump, and operated from tactical bases from 500 to 900 miles from its supply bases.*
>
> *The Liberators did many things their designers never intended. They skip-bombed ships from mast height, strafed at low-level, ferreted out enemy radar stations, mined rivers and harbors, flew transport missions, and on one occasion functioned as fighters.*
>
> *After the war, when Army Air Force Headquarters in Washington tallied the bombing accuracy of every heavy bomb group in action, I was astonished to find that the 308th led them all.*

This crew, therefore, accomplished its tasks in a very impressive aircraft that did more than it was built to do.

While the record is far from complete, I obtained the following information about the members of the original crew from two of the airmen themselves, as well as from a few of the children whose fathers are now deceased plus, of course, Marc McDonald and Jana Churchwell.

A Chain of Tragedies across Air, Land and Sea

SECOND LIEUTENANT THOREL TOLLEF "SKIP" JOHNSON, pilot. Born on September 7, 1917, he was twenty-five years old and married to Estel (Beezley) when the crew was formed at Davis-Monthan Army Air Forces Field in Arizona in 1943. Along with the other crew members, he was assigned to the Pacific Theater in China. The Casualty Questionnaire, prepared after the crewmen returned to their base following the bailout over China, lists his rank as a captain.

Following his discharge from the USAAF in 1945, he became a trooper with the Colorado State Patrol, and in 1953 he rejoined the U.S. Air Force (as it was called by then) and remained in it for the next fifteen years. He retired as a major.

According to the Department of Veterans Affairs Record Processing Center in St. Louis, Missouri, he died on March 27, 1990. There are two grave monuments in his memory at the Cedar Hill Cemetery, Paonia (Delta County), Colorado. One has the usual information found on most markers, and the other displays the name "Flying Tigers," an engraved emblem of this organization and his nickname, "Skip." A daughter, Connie Johnson, provided some of the information for this project.

SECOND LIEUTENANT GEORGE LUDLOW WHITE JR., copilot. Born in Iowa but enlisting in Richmond, Virginia, he was married to Elizabeth Young White when the crew formed. Their children included Susan White Holsworth, who died in Richmond on October 2, 2011, at the age of fifty-five; Ellen

Major Thorel "Skip" Johnson at the thirty-sixth annual Fourteenth Air Force Association Convention in Seattle, Washington, in July 1982. This photo appeared in the 1983 *Annual Pictorial Magazine of the Flying Tigers of the 14th Air Force Association*. Photographer unknown.

Yoder of Massachusetts; George L. White III of Iowa; and Carolyn MacLean White of Richmond.

After Elizabeth died, he subsequently remarried and moved from Richmond, Virginia, to Massachusetts and/or Narragansett, Rhode Island, where he died in 1995. His stepson, Mark Williams, resides (or resided) at the latter location.

SECOND LIEUTENANT PETER J. DANNHARDT, navigator. Born on July 6, 1916 (and probably the second-oldest member of this crew), he was from Brooklyn, New York. A model builder in his youth, he constructed sailing ships, battleships and planes. His interest in the latter pursuit was probably a factor when he joined the USAAF after the war began. He never married.

After entering the service, he attended the Army Air Forces Navigation Training School at Selman Field (now the Monroe Regional Airport) in Monroe, Louisiana. During the war, this facility was the largest one of its kind in the United States. He was one of the two crew members who bailed out of the doomed Liberator while it was still over the ocean.

Adam Dannhardt with nephew Peter, who lost his life after bailing out of the *Hat in the Ring* over the Santa Barbara Channel on July 4, 1943. *Family photo emailed from Marc McDonald.*

While he was never seen again, his parachute was found, according to surviving crew member Gail Vanlandingham, near the shoreline north of Santa Barbara, probably near Goleta, two or three days later.

According to one newspaper article, he was the first member of his Knights of Columbus council and the first New York City fireman (Manhattan Engine Company 15) to "make the supreme sacrifice."

Peter was named after a twenty-two-year-old uncle who was killed in action in the Ardennes Forest in France in 1918, the last year of World War I.

In a letter to my informant, Marc McDonald, Peter's great-nephew, Mike Iannotta, wrote about how devastated the family was, especially his parents, after learning about Peter's loss.

SECOND LIEUTENANT ROBERT H. "BOBBY" PROSSER, bombardier. Also from New York, he was the second missing crewman to leave the plane while it was still over the ocean. His parachute was also found in the same area mentioned above.

While his body was never found, there is a marble monument located at Fairview Cemetery, Herkimer County, New York, which reads "2nd Lieut. Robert H. Prosser, 7th Bomb Sq., 34th Bomb Gp., killed near Santa Barbara, Calif. July 4, 1943, 1920–1943."

After placing an advertisement in an issue of the *American Legion* magazine in an attempt to locate surviving crew members, I received a letter of inquiry from a family relative who declared, "I was interested in the reason for [your] looking for survivors." After explaining the purpose of the project in a responding letter and seeking his help for further information, I did not hear from him again.

According to a letter from Mike Iannotta (a relative of Peter Dannhardt's), Robert Prosser was from Remsen, New York, was an actor/director in the motion picture industry and enlisted in the U.S. Army Air Corps on December 17, 1940.

TECHNICAL SERGEANT FOSTER M. HARE, first engineer. From Baltimore, Maryland, he was twenty-two years old and single when the crew was formed in 1943.

As first engineer of the B-24E that crashed in Camuesa Canyon, he was one of the three crew members, in addition to the pilot and copilot, who wrote a statement explaining the loss of the aircraft in the Report of Aircraft Accident.

According to his individual Casualty Questionnaire, prepared when the crew members returned to their base after the bailout over China, he was heard to say, before leaving the aircraft, that the "gas supply was being exhausted."

He is buried at Glen Haven Memorial Park, Glen Burnie, Maryland.

STAFF SERGEANT BRAYDON L. HASSINGER, second engineer and ball turret gunner. From Altoona, Pennsylvania, he attended Phillipsburg High School, where he was a member of the football team. Graduating in 1941, he was a shipping clerk at a textile plant before entering the service on August 17, 1942. When the crew formed, some time after he received his gunner's wings from the Army Flexible Gunnery School at Fort Myer, Florida, he was twenty-two years old and single. He also received training at Keesler Army Airfield (now Keesler Air Force Base) in Biloxi, Mississippi, and other airfields in California, Arizona and Texas. After the airmen arrived in China, he was the first one to go on a combat mission.

Among his awards are the Distinguished Flying Cross (presented for "heroism or extraordinary achievement while participating in an aerial

Flying Tigers and CBI (China-Burma-India) patches from the Braydon Hassinger scrap album. *Photo by Jana Churchwell.*

This Blue Star (Service) flag was handmade by Braydon Hassinger's mother. Authorized by the Department of Defense, it was displayed by families who had members in the armed forces during times of war or other hostilities. If the member died during his or her service, the blue star was covered with a gold one. *Photo by Jana Churchwell.*

flight"), the Air Medal (awarded for meritorious service) with several oak leaf clusters, the Asiatic Medal with star attached and the Good Conduct Medal. He accumulated more than three hundred flying hours and completed fifty-three missions.

Like many other veterans, he was married after the war—in this case, in June 1946.

In late 1954, he was promoted to the permanent grade of technical sergeant by the air force, but for some unknown reason, his Certificate of Appointment is dated September 21, 1960.

According to the Department of Veterans Affairs Records Processing Center in St. Louis, Missouri, he died on January 12, 1983. His widow, Faye, and a daughter, Nancy Lorraine Hassinger Snow, both live in Orlando, Florida. A son, Ronald Hassinger, lives in the state of Washington and had a career in the air force.

Since only two living crew members could be located, more information about their personal histories was obtained from relatives. Pictured are Jana Churchwell, the niece of copilot and flight officer George F. Churchwell Jr., who was at the controls of a Liberator that crashed near Weed, California, in 1943; Faye Hassinger, the widow of Braydon Hassinger (one of the original members of the *Hat in the Ring* crew); and Nancy Lorraine Hassinger Snow, the Hassingers' daughter. *Photo by Stacy Churchwell.*

TECHNICAL SERGEANT JOHN D. WEDESKY, first radio operator. Born on March 12, 1921, in Collinsville, Illinois, he was single when the crew was formed in 1943. He entered the service in August 1942 and had accumulated 364 combat hours on sixty-four missions by the end of the war. Awards earned included the Distinguished Flying Cross with one oak leaf cluster, the Asiatic Pacific Ribbon with two battle stars, the Air Medal and the Good Conduct Medal, which he called the "good humor medal."

Returning to the United States from China on C-47 and C-54 transport aircraft, he flew to Washington, D.C., from Yangkai to Chabua, Agra, Karachi, Cairo, Algiers, Casablanca and the Azores. From here, he continued to Amana Beach, Florida, for some rest and relaxation and then to Scott Army Air Forces Field, Illinois; Sioux Falls, South Dakota; and Truax Army Air Forces Field, Madison, Wisconsin, where he was an instructor at a radio operator school. While stationed here, he met his future wife, and they married in 1947. They had two children, including a daughter, Donna Blake of Janesville, Wisconsin.

He was one of the two living crew members interviewed during the early years of this project. When I contacted him, he and his wife were living in Janesville, Wisconsin. During a period of time, he was a member of a Janesville group called the World War II Warbirds, which gathered at a local restaurant once a month to share not only war stories but also whatever other topics came to mind. John's sense of humor is illustrated when he told the story of running out of bombs while on a mission over India—they dropped tigers instead.

As a former radio operator, he was able to identify a picture of one intact item I found beneath a shrub at the wreck site: a group of three radios, called command sets, mounted on a single chassis. They were used for pilot-to-ground communication and also to receive landing instructions. The frequencies could be reset by the radio operator.

John died three days before terrorists destroyed the World Trade Center in New York City on September 11, 2001.

Though badly deteriorated, these battery packs remain intact and easily identifiable at the B-24E, 42-0711, wreck site. *Photo by Bob Burtness.*

This 1999 photo of John Wedesky was also emailed to me by Marc McDonald. John was one of two living survivors who helped to fill some gaps from the rest of the story via telephone conversations, tape-recorded oral histories and copies of newspaper articles about his wartime experiences. He died shortly before the terrorist attacks against the World Trade Center and the Pentagon in 2001. Photographer unknown.

SERGEANT GEORGE C. BELITSKUS SR., second radio operator and gunner. From McDonald, Pennsylvania, this twenty-eight-year-old crewman may have been the "old man" of the group as he was born in 1914. Even though he died in 1984, which was some time before I started this project, one of his sons, George C. Belitskus Jr., was located via an Eighth Air Force Historical Society membership directory, thanks to the efforts of Harold Province, a member of both the Thirty-fourth Bomb Group Association and the Eighth Air Force Historical Society. George Jr., the oldest of his four sons, sent Harold some copies of materials pertinent to his father's USAAF service. These items, cited previously, were later forwarded to me.

George Jr. and William live in McDonald and Kane, Pennsylvania, respectively. Patrick and Robert reside in Concord and San Mateo, California, respectively. Their mother, Margaret, died in 2009.

STAFF SERGEANT GAIL VANLANDINGHAM, armor (or ariel) gunner. He occupied the top turret or waist gunner positions; he was also a nose gunner on some missions.

Born in Uniontown, Kansas, on July 11, 1920, he entered the service on August 19, 1942, at Fort Leavenworth, Kansas. From here, he proceeded to St. Petersburg, Florida, for a week of indoctrination and then on to

Clearwater, Florida, for basic training. While there, he stayed in a three-story hotel (still in existence) that had an eighteen-hole golf course that the military used for a drill field.

On November 29, 1942, he was promoted to sergeant after attending gunnery school for six weeks at Fort Myers, Florida.

At the end of the year, he was sent to Hill Field (now Hill Air Force Base), not far from Salt Lake City, Utah, to attend radio school, but due to overfilled classes there, he was sent to Denver, Colorado, for armory gunnery school.

the Goleta/Santa Barbara

AIR HERITAGE MUSEUM

601 FIRESTONE RD. GOLETA, CA. 93117
(805) 683-8936

LOCKHEED F1
1918

June 28, 1996

Gail Vanlandingham
4235 E. Lake Sammamish Shore Lane SE
Issaquah, WA 98029-7442

Dear Gail:

Were you a crew member of a B-24 Liberator which crashed in our back country in July, 1943?

For nearly six years our museum has been gathering information about this event because we believe that its an important chapter in the rich aviation history of the Santa Barbara area. We are working with the Forest Service at the wreck site and plan to bring out the remnants of the wreck for public display and interpretation. Some items are in remarkably good condition, for example a group of three radio receivers which I brought out about two years ago.

The one missing aspect of our research is the stories of the crew members, not only the experiences and reflections of this particular flight but also the events that led to joining the Army Air Forces, and the 34th Bomb Group (H) experience in Mendlesham, England later.

If you are the Gail Vanlandingham we are looking for, or are related to this individual, we would greatly appreciate a response. If you need more information or clarification about what we are doing, please let me know.

Sincerely,

Robert A. Burtness

Robert A. Burtness

This letter was mailed to Gail Vanlandingham after his name was found five years after the research project began. Thanks to his unusual name, his contact information was located on an Internet people finder website. His experiences were obtained not only by telephone conversations, letters and mailed oral history tapes but also through a face-to-face interview with him at his home in Everett, Washington. This letter was scanned by Bob Burtness.

In March 1943, he returned to Hill Field and then proceeded to Davis-Monthan Field (now Davis-Monthan Air Force Base), Arizona, for B-24 gunnery training. This is where he met the other crew members.

He participated on 48 combat missions over China before returning to the United States.

On October 3, 1944, he married Helen Louise Brillhart and began a very special relationship that was to last nearly sixty years.

With the help of an Internet address directory that had more than 90 million names, his was the only match I found. After five years of working on the project, I finally located a "live one."

Robert A. Burtness
Air Heritage Museum
601 Firestone Road
Goleta, Ca. 93117

Dear Robert:

Yes I was a member of the B-24 Liberator that crashed in the area you spoke of. I believe it was July 4, 1943.

Two members of our crew lost their lives in that crash. We took off from Salinas Air Force Base early the evening before. We were on a 400 mile over water Navigation mission, and then we were to land at Bakersfield Air Force Base. We never made it.

In the opinion of officials of the Salinas Air Force Base the plane was sabotaged. We lost three other planes that night. As I recall we were about 200 miles from shore when we lost the number one engine. We turned and headed for the nearest shore line. Soon after, and while about 100 miles from shore, we lost the number two engine. Just before we reached shore we lost the number three engine. At that time the Bombardier and Navigator bailed out. They came down in the water. To me knowledge their bodies were never found. The rest of us stayed with the plane for a few minutes longer and then bailed out. No one in the aft section wanted to be the first to jump. This was our first jump. I ask them if I jumped would they follow me, they said yes. I jumped into the night, I was picked up later by the police and taken to the Sheriff's office in Santa Barbara. There, one by one, other members came in. Later that day we went back up to the wreck, picked up a few personal things, looked it over and went to the airport. There a B-17 pickup us up and flew us back to Salinas.

From there I believe we went to El Paso where we picked up two new members. Shortly after that we flew to Lincoln Nebr. for final staging and then we headed for China and the 14th Air Force where we flew missions against the Japanese. We were there for about 15 months then came home. We were forced to bail out in February 1944 in central China into Japanese Occupied territory. It took us about a month to find our way out, with the help of the Chinese people, and back to our home base.

I was an Armor Gunner and flew in the top turret and sometimes in waist gunner position. There are three members of our crew still living. We all got together many times after the war. My tail gunner, George Lawrence

---

The first page of Gail Vanlandingham's response to my letter. This breakthrough opened up new possibilities in obtaining the personal histories of the crew members. My contact with Gail also led to locating John Wedesky in Janesville, Wisconsin. This letter was scanned from the files of Bob Burtness.

and his wife Nancy and my wife and I Traveled and stayed together for about two years after we retired. George passed away a few years ago. After the Korean war I was discharged from the Air Force and went to work for the Boeing Co. and worked there for 30 years. My wife and I retired in July 1982. We now have a home here in Issaquah Washington where we spent our summers. In winter we have a home in Mesa Arizona. We are still in good heath and enjoy life very much.

We still drive to Arizona each fall and sometimes we come down through California. We might come down that way this fall and stop and see your Museum. If there is any other information I might be able to help you with let me know.

Sincerely Yours

Gail Vanlandingham

The second page of Gail Vanlandingham's response to my letter. While the Veterans Administration had no record of him, the Internet did. This letter was scanned from the files of Bob Burtness.

This photo was taken of Gail Vanlandingham at his home in Everett, Washington, in 2005. *Photo by Bob Burtness.*

Responding to my letter, he and John Wedesky enabled me to learn much about what happened to the crew after the bailout near Santa Barbara fifty-one years earlier.

After the Korean War, Gail was discharged from the air force and began a thirty-year career with the Boeing Company. Following his retirement in July 1982, he and his wife, Helen, divided their time between a home in Issaquah, Washington, during the summer and one in Mesa, Arizona, during the winter. A widower since 2003, he moved to Everett, Washington (not far from Seattle), to be closer to family members, although four of their five children, including daughter Terry (who died at the age of seven), are now deceased. He is apparently the last surviving member of the original crew.

STAFF SERGEANT GEORGE A. LAWRENCE, tail gunner. As a Utica, New York native, he was twenty years old and single when the crew was formed. He graduated from the Aviation Gunnery School in Fort Meyer, Virginia. During his later years, he and his wife, Nancy, traveled with the Vanlandinghams. He passed away some years ago.

All but two of these crewmen became members of an elite organization known as the "Caterpillar Club." A membership certificate is granted to any serviceman "whose life was spared...because of an emergency parachute jump from an aircraft." In this instance, these men performed the feat twice in two different countries—the first one friendly but the second one, occupied China, not so friendly.

Such "drop ins," it appears, were also acknowledged by the manufacturers of their parachutes. The text of the letter below was sent to Braydon Hassinger from Stanley Switlik of the Switlik Parachute Company in Trenton, New Jersey:

Dear Sir:—

We are advised that you have been accepted as a qualifying member of the CATERPILLAR CLUB, *and that your name has accordingly been added to the roster of members. The Switlik Parachute Company has the honor of presenting your credentials and insignia pin; and it is a pleasure to embrace this opportunity of congratulating you upon the fact that your life has been spared through the medium of a parachute.*

We can appreciate that the details connected with your own emergency jump proved to be very thrilling experiences for you; and your record as furnished to the Club is not only of current interest, but will serve as an everlasting memory of you personally. It may interest you to know that these records of members will be perpetually maintained in the Club Museum, now located in Trenton, and it is the purpose of the Club to extend to its members a cordial invitation to call at any time they may find it convenient to review them.

The credentials and pin are symbolic of the precepts for the promotion of air-safety and the spirit of good fellowship, which have always been maintained by the Club; and you may justifiably be proud in thus becoming affiliated with those traditions which have become internationally known during the many years since its inception.

We sincerely trust you will receive as much pleasure in accepting these credentials as we have in presenting them to you, and it is our hope that you

Scanned copy of a letter to Sergeant Braydon Hassinger from the Switlik Parachute Company in Trenton, New Jersey. While the letter advised that he had been accepted as a member of the Caterpillar Club, thus verifying that he had parachuted from an aircraft under emergency conditions, this was the second time that he had done so. The first time was over Santa Barbara in early July of the previous year.

89

may enjoy many more hours of uninterrupted flying service; and that should the occasion ever arise when your life depends on a similar emergency, you will again have a parachute for your protection.

While there is no mention of a product guarantee in this letter, I presume that the company would provide a free replacement if the first one failed for any reason.

Returning to the serious nature of this crew's missions, it must be recognized that the men's accomplishments, especially surviving numerous crises during the war, can undoubtedly be attributed in major part to working as a team. While a typical crew consists of four officers and six enlisted men, and fraternizing between the two groups is generally frowned on, these individuals did virtually everything together. They trained and flew the missions together, and each of them depended on the others to

This is a copy of a Caterpillar Club membership certificate awarded to Sergeant Braydon Hassinger after he bailed out of a Liberator during a mission over China in early 1944.

accomplish the critical tasks at hand. When they were forced to bail out of the stricken aircraft in darkness, they had to look out for one another just to make it through the night.

During the second bailout, also at night, they found themselves in an unknown territory occupied by the enemy, and they were obligated to work together along an uncertain path that would hopefully lead to a successful escape from possible capture and death.

This mission also had three airmen who were not members of the original crew. They included Sergeant Charles A. Dealy (gunner), First Lieutenant John E. Bush (bombardier) and First Lieutenant Howard M. Kirkland (navigator).

According to the Individual Casualty Questionnaire, two of them experienced injuries, apparently not too serious, after bailing out of the aircraft. Lieutenant Kirkland's back was slightly wrenched when his parachute opened, and Sergeant Dealy acquired a pulled leg muscle when he landed. All three are shown in the "walkout photo" taken at the end of their twenty-three-day ordeal in China.

Sergeant Charles A. Dealy, gunner, was a member of the Johnson crew when the men had to bail out while returning from a mission to Thailand. This photo was probably taken at their base in Yangkai, China.

Replacement navigator First Lieutenant Howard M. Kirkland was with the Johnson crew when it bailed out over China in 1944. Surviving the war along with the other members on that mission, he is buried at the Salisbury National Cemetery in North Carolina. *Photo by Jana Churchwell.*

Lieutenant Kirkland, born on January 1, 1921, died on January 30, 1981, and is buried with his wife, Connie, at the Salisbury National Cemetery in North Carolina.

Lieutenant Bush, was born in Lowville, New York, on November 29, 1916, and attended local schools before serving in the USAAF between 1941 and 1945. Among his awards was the Distinguished Flying Cross. Returning to Lowville after the war, he owned two local businesses before retiring in 1978. He died in March 1990 at the age of seventy-three.

The Wreck Sites Today

SAN MIGUEL ISLAND

Until recent years, San Miguel Island was managed by the navy, and access to it was very difficult. Now it is controlled by the National Park Service, and while it is accessible to the public for hiking and camping on a reservation basis, users are obligated to stay on designated trails and other areas.

While visiting the plane wreck site may be a possibility, it would have to be done by reservation and only when a ranger is available for escort through a sensitive habitat to get there. As is the case with any archaeological site, none of the artifacts can be removed from here.

Many years ago, while the navy still had jurisdiction over the island, larger pieces of the wreckage, such as the intact twin tail assembly, were dynamited. The purpose of this "additional disassembly process" was to decrease the possibility of the wreck being reported again as an undiscovered one. This act also "disassembled" some history.

While numerous photographs were taken at both wreck sites, the ones selected for publication focus on identifiable parts of these aircraft.

In spite of the violent forces present when airplanes slam into hillsides, often resulting in explosions and fires, it is amazing that some of the smaller parts survive remarkably intact. Others, also fabricated with high-quality aluminum or stainless steel, become fascinating yet bizarre sculptures twisted into a variety of grotesque shapes.

Regardless of what they look like after impact, however, their appearances do change over time. For example, two different photos of the throttle control

This view shows Green Mountain on San Miguel Island. At an elevation of 831 feet, it is the highest point on the island. B-24, 42-7160, crashed to the left of the summit. *Photo by Marc McDonald.*

Above: Propeller at the wreck site of B-24E, 42-7160, on San Miguel Island. This aircraft was listed as missing until it was discovered eight months later by two sailors stationed on the island. *Courtesy of Duncan Abbott.*

Opposite bottom: Shown here is part of the instrument panel from the San Miguel Island wreckage. *Photo by Marc McDonald.*

A Chain of Tragedies across Air, Land and Sea

This propeller, from the San Miguel Island B-24 wreck, was photographed many years after another picture was taken of a different propeller from the same wreck. The latter image shows the propeller mostly covered by the encroaching vegetation. *Photo by Marc McDonald.*

Three cylinders from one of the San Miguel Island B-24's engines. Each of the four Pratt & Whitney R-1830 radial engines had two rows of seven cylinders and produced 1,200 horsepower. *Photo by Marc McDonald.*

Throttle control console of B-24E, 42-7160, San Miguel Island. *Courtesy of Duncan Abbott.*

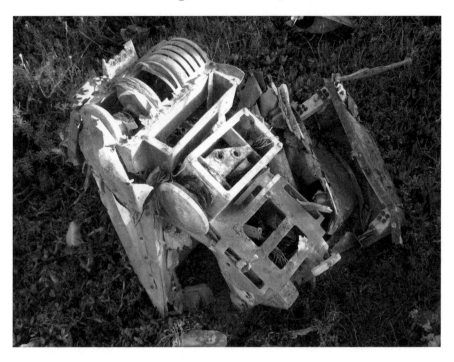

The same console, photographed decades later, shows the effects that the sun, sand and salt air produced over time. *Photo by Marc McDonald.*

console, shown above and on the opposite page, were taken decades apart, thus illustrating the combined effects produced by the sun, wind and salt air.

But these are not the only changes occurring at wreck sites. Life sprung from death in numerous South Pacific lagoons when abundant varieties of marine organisms were spawned on sunken ships, aircraft and other machines of war after the hostilities ceased.

Similarly, a plethora of colorful vegetation crowded around the remnants of the bomber on San Miguel Island where twelve airmen perished in 1943.

LOS PADRES NATIONAL FOREST

It was perhaps during the early 1970s when most of the *Hat in the Ring/ Eddie Rickenbacker* was hauled away and recycled. There is evidence of a rudimentary access route leading from an old firebreak that connects with a national forest road. While much of this road is publicly accessible via ORV, horses and hikers, it is not open to other traffic such as cars and trucks.

Fragment from the left wing of B-24E, 42-0711, the *Hat in the Ring*. This item is currently on display in the Commemorative Air Force's Southern California Wing Museum at the Camarillo Airport. *Photo by Marc McDonald.*

One of the main landing gears of the *Hat in the Ring* reposing in one of the few clear areas of the chaparral-covered hillside. *Photo by Bob Burtness.*

Bomb bay door of B-24E, 42-0711. When retracted, these flexible pocket doors disappeared into the fuselage. *Photo by Bob Burtness.*

The wreck site is difficult to find as it is well covered with chaparral, and the remaining remnants are not easy to see until one is almost on top of them. I was equipped with a better camera during my last visit but lacked the loppers that would have facilitated moving around the site. That part of it is on a steep hillside makes the outing even more challenging and, of course, exciting.

Nevertheless, I have noted the "mysterious disappearance" of at least two types of artifacts of interest since my first visit to the main crash site. Aside from souvenir hunters, there are individuals and companies that retrieve usable parts from aircraft wrecks in order to sell them, at the highest possible prices, to vintage airplane restorers.

This area, too, is now protected under the national forest's Heritage Resources Program, even though some forest service personnel, over the years, have stated that airplane wrecks should be removed in the interest of "cleaning up the forest." This view is supported by the fact that old wrecks are sometimes mistakenly identified as new crashes by search-and-rescue personnel.

Crew member's seat, B-24E, 42-0711. The darkened portions suggest evidence of the fire caused by the impact of the crash against the hillside. *Photo by Bob Burtness.*

One of the B-22 turbo-compressors (superchargers) found at the wreck site of B-24E, 42-0711. It was powered by the engine exhaust. *Photo by Bob Burtness.*

Nose landing gear of B-24E, 42-0711. *Photo by Bob Burtness.*

Possibly one of the bomb shackles from B-24E, 42-0711. While fire scars are still evident here, these items are among the shiniest at the wreck site. *Photo by Bob Burtness.*

Armor plating was installed in strategic areas of the aircraft to help protect crew members from flak and other incoming ordnance. This particular example, found at the 42-0711 wreck site, measures 9 inches wide, 22½ inches long and ½ an inch thick. Weighing about thirty pounds, it appears to be intact, with no damage caused by the crash. The painted letters of the mounting instructions, "5 FACE TO BE INSTALLED AWAY FROM CREW," are still visible, even after long exposure to the elements. *Photo by Bob Burtness.*

On the other hand, there are others who believe that such wreck sites, especially the older ones, have become landmarks of sorts and should therefore be left alone. In the words of one search-and-rescue pilot, "They're monuments to someone's bad luck or poor judgment."

In Memoriam

To those fourteen crew members whose lives were lost in (or from) two Liberators that crashed in Santa Barbara County, we recall and honor their service to their country. While these losses were not in combat, they were in training, directly or indirectly, for combat. All of them were preparing to face an enemy that threatened the very existence of our nation. They were preparing to go into battle, not as conquerors but as liberators, to allow the subdued peoples of other countries to determine their own destinies rather than be subjected to the whims of dictators making such decisions for them.

B-24E, 42-7160

The name, if any, is unknown. Many of the aircraft used for training purposes did not have names at this stage but rather acquired them when the crews arrived at their combat staging areas later.

Flight Officer Vernon Clarke Stevens (pilot)

First Lieutenant Douglas J. Thornburg (command/instructor pilot)*

Second Lieutenant Noah Hoseah Yost (bombardier)

Staff Sergeant Ralph S. Masterson (assistant engineer)

Lieutenant Thornburg in his pilot's uniform. This photo, too, was probably taken by a professional. Photographer unknown.

Staff Sergeant Bernard Littman (engineer)

Staff Sergeant Walter O. Eisenbarth (gunner)

Second Lieutenant Bose Gorman (gunner)

Staff Sergeant Lee E. Salzer (gunner)

Staff Sergeant Henry L. Bair (assistant radioman)

Staff Sergeant Lyle L. Frost (radioman)

Second Lieutenant Justin M. Marshall (bombardier instructor)

Second Lieutenant Floyd P. Hart (copilot)

In Memoriam

*Just three weeks before this tragic ending, Lieutenant Thornburg, age twenty-five, was the command/instructor pilot of a B-24 that crashed on June 10, 1943, in Weed, California (Siskiyou County), near Mount Shasta during a nighttime navigation training flight, also from the Salinas Army Air Base. He was one of four survivors who successfully parachuted from the disabled aircraft. The six other crewmen died in the crash. While his role was that of the aircraft commander and instructor and not the pilot flying the aircraft, his statement in the Report of Aircraft Accident, after the first crash, indicates that he was involved in attempting to help keep the aircraft in the air as long as possible while looking for a place to land or getting everyone out of the plane if that were not possible.

His statement of June 11, 1943, appears as follows:

Takeoff was approximately 2350, June 9, 1943. We climbed to 11,000 feet and proceeded on course with no undue occurrence until, approximately 0200. At approximately 0200 we had a drop of manifold pressure on all four engines, the inter-cooler shutters were closed and the manifold pressure returned to normal.

Shortly thereafter, at approximately 0215, the oil pressure on number two engine began to oscillate. We did not feather the engine immediately, but watched the cylinder head and oil temperature gauges. Both temperature gauges remained normal for the next few minutes, and we thought it possible that the oil pressure gauge was at fault. Then sparks began emanating from the cowlings of number two engine and the oil pressure dropped to twenty (20) pounds or less. The Pilot then cut off the super-charger, retarded the throttle, placed the propeller in full high pitch and attempted to feather the engine. The engine would not feather. I made several unsuccessful attempts to feather the engine and noticed blue sparks reflecting in the windshield behind the feather button.

At this time the Pilot increased the R.P.M. to 2500 and the manifold pressure to something over 40 inches on the three good engines. The vacuum selector valve had been changed from number two engine to number one engine a few minutes previous. Number two engine began to vibrate considerably. I had all crew members put parachutes on at this time. The Pilot called the Navigator and asked him where we were. The Navigator said we were over Redding—actually we were approximately thirty (30) or fourty [sic] (40) miles north of Redding. The Pilot told the Navigator to put his parachute on and told him that we were going to look for a place to land.

We started a turn to see if we could locate Redding; no air port [sic] was visible. While we were turning, number two engine feathered itself.

This stopped the vibration and I decided to return to Sacramento. I told the Pilot to get out and let me get in the Pilot's seat. At this time he was still adjusting his parachute and did not leave the seat immediately. Our turn was being made very gradually to the left as there were mountains to the right and ahead of us. We had lost some altitude probably down to 10,000 feet, by this time. I looked out the Pilot's window and noticed that number one engine was feathered. I asked the Pilot and Co-Pilot if either of them had feathered number one; each of them said he had not. I attempted to un-feather number one and it began to turn. I don't remember the exact R.P.M. at which I pulled the button out, however, the next time I looked at the engine it was feathered again. I made several more attempts to unfeather [sic] number one with no success. While working with number one feather button I again noticed blue sparks reflecting in the windshield behind the feather button. We tried using the circuit breaker buttons in conjunction with the feather button, but with no better results.

We had now finished our turn and were headed south. Both engineers had gone to the rear section to inform the men we were in trouble and to help them with their parachutes. Just about the time I stopped trying to unfeather [sic] number one engine everything electrical—lights, instruments, etc., went out. I told the bombardier, who was standing behind me, to open the bomb-bay doors—then I attempted to ring the alarm bell, I could not hear it ring and feel sure it did not ring.

The bombardier had some trouble opening the bomb-bay doors, but finally opened them at approximately 6,000 feet indicated. I told him and the radio operator to jump. The bombardier had a flashlight which he flashed at the men in the rear section and jumped with the flashlight still on. The radio operator jumped immediately afterward.

The Pilot by now was out of his seat. I asked the Co-Pilot [George F. Churchwell Jr.] if he had the ship under control and he replied that he did. The Co-Pilot was very calm the entire time and was holding the ship on an even keel, although we were losing altitude rather rapidly. The Pilot jumped and I told the Co-Pilot that everyone was out and that it was time to leave. He asked me to make sure and I told him I was sure as far as I could tell. He unbuckled his safety-belt and left his seat, as he started between the seats I went to the bomb-bay and jumped. I waited several seconds and pulled the ripcord. Almost immediately after my chute opened the ship hit the ground and burst into flame. I landed a few seconds later about two hundred yards from the ship. I removed my chute and went to the ship—it took me five or six minutes to reach the ship as the under-

brush was quite thick in the vicinity. When I did reach the ship four or five civilians were present. They were removing Sgt. Kennedy from the wreckage, he was hanging on the outside with his parachute caught in the waist door opening. I helped them drag his body away and could see one other body in the ship. One of the civilians took me to Weed, California, in his car and I called Salinas Army Air Base.

It is my opinion that the two engineers and tail gunner were attempting to free Kennedy's parachute when the ship crashed.

Due to the urgency of the moment, it is possible that Sergeant Kennedy may have "popped" his parachute just before, or just after, leaving the plane. At any rate, not enough time was allowed to make sure that the chute was clear of the aircraft.

B-24E, 42-7011 (*HAT IN THE RING/EDDIE RICKENBACKER*)

Second Lieutenant Peter J. Dannhardt (navigator)

Second Lieutenant Robert E. Prosser (bombardier)

Appendix II
Lieutenant Thornburg and the Crew of Another Liberator

The story of another Liberator, B-24E, 42-7119, which crashed in Weed, California, on June 10, 1943, during a training mission, is not related to the Liberators cited in the first appendix, but its crewmen were also in the Second Air Force, and they were stationed at the same installation, Salinas Army Air Base. Further, one of these crew members was command/instructor pilot First Lieutenant Douglas J. Thornburg, whose story appears earlier and in the coming pages.

FLIGHT OFFICER GEORGE F. CHURCHWELL, copilot. He was the last one flying the aircraft just before it crashed. Wanting to make sure that everyone had already bailed out, he then left his seat and headed toward an exit but died in the ensuing crash.

SECOND LIEUTENANT GEORGE HYDE CLARKE JR., navigator. He died in the crash of this plane. As an interesting part of the family history, his mother, her sister and brother, plus his grandmother, all survived the *Titanic* disaster of 1912, but his sister, WASP Susan Parker Clarke, was one of thirty-eight WASPs (Women's Airforce Service Pilot) killed when her plane crashed in 1944.

SECOND LIEUTENANT ALFRED J. DEMEUSY, pilot. He was one of the four crew members who successfully bailed out of the ship.

STAFF SERGEANT WILLET F. DRAKER, engineer. He was killed when this plane crashed.

Flight officer George F. Churchwell Jr. was at the controls of a Liberator when it crashed near Weed, California, on June 10, 1943. The command/instructor pilot on that training mission survived but died three weeks later in a Liberator crash on San Miguel Island. *Courtesy of Jana Churchwell.*

SERGEANT ALVIN DSCHAAK, radio operator. While he was one of the four crewmen who successfully parachuted from the plane during a training mission over Weed, California, he died six months later while serving as a replacement nose turret gunner on a mission over Europe. The ship was rammed by a damaged BF 109G-2 flown by a Bulgarian pilot, who was also killed.

STAFF SERGEANT ALONZIA E. "EARL" JOHNSTON, gunner. He died in the crash.

SERGEANT JOHN F. "JACK" KENNEDY, gunner. While attempting to bail out from the aircraft, his parachute snagged in the waist door opening, and he was trapped. As a result, he was killed when the plane crashed. Two other crew members, including Staff Sergeant William W. Powell Jr., also died while attempting to help him break free of the falling aircraft.

STAFF SERGEANT WILLIAM WARREN POWELL JR., assistant engineer. He was fatally injured in the crash while attempting to help Sergeant Kennedy bail out of the plane.

FIRST LIEUTENANT DOUGLAS J. THORNBURG, command/instructor pilot. He was one of four crew members who successfully bailed out of this stricken aircraft (see his Report of Aircraft Accident statement cited previously), but he and eleven others died three weeks later when their Liberator, looking for Lieutenants Dannhardt and Prosser, crashed on San Miguel Island.

SECOND LIEUTENANT CHARLES LINCOLN "CHUCK" WIEST SR., bombardier. One of the four crew members to successfully parachute from this plane, he later had to jump from a burning Liberator, hit by flak, on a mission over Germany on April 8, 1944. On the way down, he and copilot Lieutenant Leroy M. Williamson witnessed the murder of their pilot, Lieutenant Guy Johnson, already on the ground, by German soldiers. Lieutenant Wiest spent the remainder of the war in a POW camp at Stalag Luft 1. He survived the war.

Bibliography

BOOKS

Ambrose, Stephen E. *The Wild Blue: The Men and Boys Who Flew the B-24's Over Germany, 1944–1945.* New York: Simon & Shuster, 2002.

Bergstrom, Dennis D. *Gallant Warriors: Propeller-Driven Warbird Fighter and Bomber Survivors Around the World.* Spokane, WA: D.D. Bergstrom, 1993.

Cass, William F. *The Last Flight of Liberator 41-1133: The Lives, Times, Training and Loss of the Bomber Crew Which Crashed on Trail Peak at Philmont Scout Ranch.* Ashland, OH: Winds Aloft Press, 1996.

Chennault, Claire L. *Way of a Fighter: The Memoirs of Claire Lee Chennault.* New York: G.P. Putnam's Sons, 1949.

Childers, Thomas. *Wings of Morning: The Story of the Last American Bomber Shot Down Over Germany in World War II.* New York: Addison-Wesley Publishing, 1995.

Emde, Heiner. *Conquerors of the Air: The Evolution of Aircraft 1903–1945.* Illustrated by Carlo Demand. New York: Bonanza Books, 1968.

Freeman, Roger A. *B-17 Fortress at War.* New York: Charles Scribner's Sons, 1977.

Glines, Carroll V. *Chennault's Forgotten Warriors: The Saga of the 308th Bomb Group in China*. Atglen, PA: Schiffer Publishing, Ltd., 1995.

Haynes, Elmer E., and A.B. Feurer. *The B-24 in China: General Chennault's Secret Weapon in WWII*. Mechanicsburg, PA: Stackpole Military History Series, 2006.

Hillenbrand, Laura. *Unbroken: A World War II Story of Survival, Resilience and Redemption*. New York: Random House, 2010.

Livingstone, William R. *Remembering World War II: The POW Stories*. Santa Barbara, CA: self-published, 2009.

Macha, Gary P. "Pat," and Don Jordan. *Aircraft Wrecks in the Mountains of California, 1909–2002*. 3rd edition. Lake Forest, CA: Info Net Publishing, 2002.

Mathews, John, and Nancy Robinson Masters. *Spirits in the Sky: The Airplanes of World War II*. Photographs from the Collection of the Confederate (now Commemorative) Air Force. Dallas, TX: Taylor Publishing, 1990.

Maurer, Maurer, ed. *Air Force Combat Units of World War II*. Washington, D.C.: Office of Air Force History, 1983.

———. *Combat Squadrons of the Air Force, World War II*. USAF Historical Division, Air University, Department of the Air Force, 1969.

McDowell, Ernest R. *Flying Fortress: The Boeing B-17*. Illustrated by Don Greer. Carrollton, TX: Squadron/Signal Publications, 1987.

Nutter, Ralph H. *With the Possum and the Eagle: The Memoir of a Navigator's War Over Germany and Japan*. Novato, CA: Presidio Press, Inc., 2002.

O'Leary, Michael, Norman Pealing and Mike Jerram. *Warbirds: Classic American Fighters and Bombers*. New York: Military Press, 1990.

Smith, Starr. *Jimmy Stewart: Bomber Pilot*. St. Paul, MN: Zenith Press, 2005.

Thomas, Rowan T. *Born in Battle: Round the World Adventures of the 513th Bombardment Squadron*. Philadelphia, PA: John C. Winston Company, 1944.

Tompkins, Walker A. *Goleta the Good Land*. Goleta, CA: Goleta Amvets Post No. 55, 1966.

————. *It Happened in Old Santa Barbara*. Santa Barbara, CA: Santa Barbara National Bank, 1976.

NEWSPAPER ARTICLES

Casa Grande (AZ) Dispatch. "Find Flyer's Body on San Miguel Isle: B-24 and 12 Airmen Missing Since July; Lt. Thornburg Killed." March 24, 1944.

Daunt, Tina. "Firm Hopes to Salvage Wrecks of Warplanes." *Los Angeles Times*, undated.

Fordyce, Sam. "Once Upon a Time at Ellwood." *Santa Barbara News-Press*, April 17, 2012, A-6.

Kieding, Bob. "Bombing of Ellwood Key to Japanese-American Internment." *Santa Barbara News-Press*, April 4, 2012, A-2.

————. "Is the Montebello a Ticking Time Bomb?" *Santa Barbara News-Press*, January 18, 2012, A-2.

Los Angeles Times. "Plane Crash 11 Years Ago Linked to Sea Tragedy." Sunday, October 3, 1954.

[Newspaper unknown]. "Tortuous Line Supplies Yank Fliers in China." No date.

[Newspaper unknown but possibly one in his hometown, Altoona, Pennsylvania]. "Hassinger Writes Letter from China: Bomber Outfit is Getting Crack at Japs." January 20, 1944.

Santa Barbara News-Press. "Base Identifies Missing Fliers." July 13, 1943, B-1.

————. "Search for Two Flyers Continues." July 6, 1943, A-1.

————. "Two Missing Flyers Sought in Air Crash." July 5, 1943, A-1.

Schwartz, Noaki. "State Officials: No Environmental Risk from WWII Ship: Oil Tanker Was Torpedoed by a Japanese Sub in 1941." *Santa Barbara News-Press*, October 22, 2011.

Utica Observer Dispatch. "Hunt Ends for Remsen Air Officer." Wednesday, July 13, 1943, 4-A.

Walker, James, Technical Sergeant. "Combat Vet Jumped from B-24 to Safety on Mountain in China." Unidentified newspaper published by the Army Air Forces Training Command, Friday, April 6, 1945.

MAGAZINE ARTICLES

Koch, R.W. "California's Bad Luck Bombers." *Briefing: Journal of the International B-24 Liberator Club* (Fall 1987): 1–3.

O'Connell, Karra. "World War II: The Golden Age of Nose Art." *The Dispatch: The Official Magazine of the Commemorative Air Force* 36, no. 7 (July 2011): 22.

Richart, Raymond W. "Los Padres National Forest Now; Santa Barbara National Forest 65 Years Ago." *Los Padres Notes* 1, no. 1 (1981): 10–11. Los Padres Interpretive Association, Inc.

MAGAZINES

Annual Pictorial Magazine of the Flying Tigers of the 14th Air Force Association, 1989.

MEMORANDA

C.H. Fogg, Major, U.S. Air Force. Memorandum for Director, Flight Safety Research. Subject: B-24 Accident, September 29, 1954.

LETTERS

All letters to author unless otherwise noted.

Belitskus, George C., Staff Sergeant, United States Army Air Forces, A.S.N. 33290801, 373 Bomb Squadron, A.P.O. 627, to brother, Frank, and sister-in-law, c/o New York, New York, November 15, 1943.

Clapper, John R., Colonel, USAF, Commander, Department of the Air Force, Headquarters Air Force Safety Agency, Kirtland Air Force Base, New Mexico, January 28, 1994.

Clark, John J., Jr., Chief, Reports Division, Department of the Air Force, Headquarters Air Force Safety Center, Kirtland Air Force Base, New Mexico, February 7, 1996.

Gillespie, Richard E., Executive Director, International Group for Historic Aircraft Recovery (TIGHAR), September 10, 1992.

Hagedorn, Dan, Archives Division, Mail Code 322, National Air and Space Museum, Smithsonian Institution, April 26, 1993.

Hallet, Jeff D., Disposal Policy, Directorate of Logistics, Headquarters Air Force Materiel Command, Department of the Air Force, Wright-Patterson Air Force Base, Ohio, March 22, 1993.

Hunter, Alice I., Chief, Field Servicing Division, Records Processing Center, Department of Veterans Affairs, St. Louis, Missouri, September 21, 1995.

Iannotta, Mike, great-nephew of Peter Dannhardt, to Marc McDonald, March 6, 2006.

Love, William C., Lieutenant Colonel, USAF, Chief, Special Litigation Branch, General Litigation Division, Air Force Legal Services Agency, Arlington, Virginia, April 30, 1996.

Pontes, Patrick G., Ranger, Santa Barbara District, Los Padres National Forest, December 20, 1991.

Province, Harold E., Treasurer, Thirty-fourth Bomb Group Association, July 17, 1993.

————, August 2, 1993.

Richart, Raymond W., May 3, 1993.

Simpson, Robert M., June 5, 1993.

Switlik, Stanley, probably the president of the Switlik Parachute Company, to Braydon L. Hassinger, April 10, 1944.

Vanlandingham, Gail, December 2, 1996.

————, letter undated but the envelope is postmarked July 2, 1996.

————, September 10, 1996.

REPORTS

AFPPA-11, "Individual Casualty Questionnaire," Headquarters Fourteenth Air Force, undated but probably written in late February or early March 1944 after the bailout over China. This form was used for all of the crew members with the exception of the aircraft commander, Captain Johnson. The unnumbered questions are in the third person, and Captain Johnson responded to them. Many of his answers are the same for each crew member in regard to what happened after the bailout.

AFPPA-12, "Casualty Questionnaire," Headquarters Fourteenth Air Force, undated but probably prepared in late February or early March 1944 after the bailout over China. This form was filled in by Captain Johnson only and has fourteen questions for his responses. Examples ask if the crew members bailed out, where the aircraft struck the ground, who was in the aircraft when it did and their condition.

Individual Fire Report, Santa Barbara Ranger District, Los Padres National Forest, July 6, 1943.

Koch, R.W. *A Report: U.S. Army Air Corps B-24 "Liberator" Bomber Crash on San Miguel Island—July 5, 1943*, September, 1984.

War Department, U.S. Army Air Forces. Report of Aircraft Accident (B-24E, Serial No. 42-7119), June 10, 1943.

———. Report of Aircraft Accident (B-24E, Serial No. 42-7011), July 4, 1943. See the note at the end of the bibliography regarding this report.

———. Report of Missing Aircraft (B-24E, Serial No. 42-7160), July 5, 1943.

MAPS

U.S. Department of Agriculture, Forest Service. *Public Camping Areas in Santa Barbara County and Portions of Ventura County*, 1950. Modifications by Canalino Lodge No. 90, Order of the Arrow, Mission Council, Boy Scouts of America, Santa Barbara, California, Robert A. Burtness, Chairman, Camping Booklet Committee, 1961.

VIDEOS

Great Planes. Series 1, vol. 7, *B-24 Liberator.* VHS, Aeroco, Inc., 1989.

DIRECTORIES

Santa Barbara City Directories, 1941–48. Los Angeles, CA: Santa Barbara Directory Company.

~

Note: I received two different versions of this report. A cover letter, dated January 28, 1994, accompanied the first one and explained that the report included only the releasable portions because:

a. The safety investigating board analysis, findings, and recommendations are exempt from disclosure under the United States Code, Title 5, Section 552(b) (5), and Air Force Regulation (AFR) 4-33, paragraph 15e. Release of this information would have a stifling effect on the free and frank expression of ideas and opinions of Air Force officials.

b. The statements of witnesses giving unsworn testimony before the safety investigating board, as well as any direct or implied references to such testimony, are exempt from disclosure under the United States Code, Title 5, Section 552(b)(f5), and AFR 4-33, paragraph 15e. In order to promote full disclosure, witnesses are promised by the mishap investigation board that their testimony will be used solely for mishap prevention and for no other purpose. This promise of confidentiality is made in order to encourage witnesses to disclose to the investigating board everything they know about the mishap even though the statements they make may be against their personal interest or possibly incriminating.

Release of these portions of the safety report, even though the report is old, would jeopardize a significant government interest by inhibiting its ability to conduct future safety investigations of Air Force aircraft mishaps. Disclosure of this information would be contrary to the promises of confidentiality extended to witnesses and investigators. There was no time limit placed on this promise, and such a disclosure could set a precedent that would result in a weakening of the process whereby the Air Force gathers and evaluates safety information in future aircraft mishaps. Witnesses and investigators would be less candid if they knew that at some future date what they said would be released outside of safety channels. The decreased ability of the Air Force to gather and evaluate safety information would result in the increased loss of aircraft and crewmembers and ultimately have a detrimental effect on national security.

Should you decide that an appeal to this decision is necessary, you must write to the Secretary of the Air Force within 60 calendar days from the date of this letter. Include in the appeal your reasons for reconsideration and attach a copy of this letter.

I did that and received a complete copy of the report, dated February 7, 1996, just over two years later. About two and a half months after that, I received a letter from the Air Force Legal Services Agency (AFLSA), advising that a full copy of the safety report in question had been released to me.

It appears that the lesson here is to be patient but determined. I have the impression that individuals requesting such reports nowadays do not have to wait two years to get them.

Index

About the Author

R obert A. "Bob" Burtness was born in Santa Barbara, California and attended local public schools before completing a bachelor's degree at Claremont Men's College (now Claremont McKenna College).

Upon graduation, he joined the air force and spent most of a five-year period as a supply and logistics officer in Greece and New Jersey. Following separation from the service in 1966, he attended graduate schools at what is now called Chico State University and California Polytechnic University at San Luis Obispo and earned an MA in English from the latter institution.

Robert A. "Bob" Burtness. *Photograph by Olan Mills Church Directories.*

He spent the next thirty years as a teacher in the Santa Barbara secondary school system, followed by flunking retirement and continuing as a substitute, mostly in private schools.

Other activities include Boy Scout summer camp staff positions in nature, aquatics and bugling; a volunteer wilderness ranger with the forest service; volunteer projects with the Nature Conservancy on Santa Cruz Island; Commemorative Air Force oral history interviews; driving a miniature train at the Goleta Depot; toy train collecting; swimming, hiking and bicycling; and reading and writing.

He and his wife, Lynn, whom he has known since the ninth grade, live in a longtime family home rebuilt into a Queen Anne/Victorian. Both widowed some time ago, they are the parents of three adult daughters. The family in residence now consists of two cats and a variety of wildlife in the surrounding urban forest.